The True Adventures of
GRIZZLY ADAMS

JAMES CAPEN ADAMS

When he related his adventures to Theodore Hittell in San Francisco in the late 1850s, John "Grizzly" Adams used the name printed above. The portrait was drawn from life by Charles Nahl.

The True Adventures of
GRIZZLY ADAMS

A Biography by
Robert M. McClung

MORROW JUNIOR BOOKS
NEW YORK

FOR GALE

ILLUSTRATIONS CREDITS: p. 9: Courtesy, American Antiquarian Society, Worcester, Massachusetts. p. 179: From Barnum, *Struggles and Triumphs* (1875). p. 4: Barnum Museum, Bridgeport, Connecticut. p. 38: Cover of Volume I, No. 11 of Beadle's Boy's Library. pp. 3, 22, 118, 127: From William Cullen Bryant, ed., *Picturesque America: The Land We Live In* (1872). p. 166: Courtesy, California Historical Society, San Francisco. pp. ii, 51, 57, 62, 74, 107, 138, 150, 158: Illustrations by Charles Nahl for Hittell, *The Adventures of James Capen Adams* (1860). p. 171: Reproduced by permission of the Huntington Library, San Marino, California. p. 18: From Hamilton Wright Mabie, *A New History of the United States* (1898). p. 23: Illustration by Frank Marryat for *Mountains and Molehills* (1855). pp. 20, 28, 130: Illustration and maps by Robert M. McClung. p. 96: Courtesy, New York Public Library, New York, New York. pp. 143, 147: Courtesy, New York State Library, Albany, New York.

Library of Congress Cataloging in Publication Data: McClung Robert M.   The true adventures of Grizzly Adams.   Bibliography: p.   Includes index.   Summary: Recounts the adventures of the nineteenth-century frontier hunter, with an emphasis on his experiences with bears. 1. Adams, Grizzly, 1812-1860—Juvenile literature. 2. Trappers—California—Biography—Juvenile literature. 3. Hunters—California—Biography—Juvenile literature. 4. Animal trainers—United States—Biography—Juvenile literature. 5. California—Biography—Juvenile literature. 6. Bear hunting—West (U.S.)—History—19th century—Juvenile literature. 7. Grizzly bear—History—19th century—Juvenile literature. 8. Trapping—West (U.S.)—History—19th century—Juvenile literature. [1. Adams, Grizzly, 1812-1860. 2. Hunters. 3. Bear hunting—West (U.S.)—History] F864.A39M38 1985   978'.02'0924   [92]   85-8886
 ISBN 0-688-05794-2

Contents

Foreword

John Adams—also known as Grizzly Adams, Old Grizzly, the Wild Yankee Hunter, and by other equally colorful names—was a man whose character, special qualities, and accomplishments made him stand out in a time (the mid-1800s) and a place (Goldrush California) noted for rugged individualists. Adams was a nonconformist, a loner by nature. He disliked the hypocrisies of civilization and society, yet struggled unceasingly to compete in that system and conquer it. His real love was the wilderness, where he could deal in his own way with life and survival.

Born and brought up near Boston, John Adams experienced a typical New England boyhood and young manhood. He had a good education, as evidenced by his general knowledge and eloquent style. Upright and fair in his dealings with others, he was quick to resent any infringement upon what he considered his own rights. He firmly believed in the prevailing view of nineteenth-century America that God had created the birds of the air and the beasts of the

field—in fact the whole of the earth and its natural goodness—for the sole use and benefit of man.

Grizzly Adams loved to hunt and trap. Over the years he
killed a great many animals, but he killed them for food or
for their furs and hides. He hated waste and considered his
actions as natural as those of a mountain lion or wolf that
killed a deer and ate its flesh. He was certainly no conserva-
tionist as the term is used today, but he genuinely loved and
appreciated wildlife and unspoiled nature, and decried the
encroachments made on it by civilized man.

Adams killed many grizzly bears, yet made faithful pets
and companions of others. He was courageous to the point
of recklessness, loyal to his friends, by turns cruel and
thoughtless, kind and generous. "He was brave," his friend
Phineas T. Barnum noted, "and with his bravery there was
enough of the romantic in his nature to make him a real
hero." Like any individual, he was a mixture of many different qualities and must be considered within the context of
his own times.

The account of his life that follows omits many of his exploits in the western mountains to concentrate on the main
sweep of his expeditions and his experiences with bears. The
story is true, with perhaps just a touch of the larger-than-life
detail that Grizzly was fond of adding when recalling his
many adventures.

1

I Have Been Beaten to a Jelly

Judging by his appearance, the man was completely out of place in New York City; he would have been much more at home in the wilderness. A bit over medium height, wiry and muscular, he wore a mountain man's ragged outfit: a buckskin coat and pantaloons fringed along the seams and pockets, and decorated with the tails of weasels and other small animals. He sported a long white beard that waved in the breeze, and a wild shock of long gray hair stuck out like straw from beneath a peculiar-looking headpiece made from the skin of a wolf's head and shoulders with several small furry tails hanging from it.

The time was mid-April 1860, and John Adams had just arrived in New York from California, after a three-and-a-half month trip around Cape Horn in the clipper ship *Golden Fleece.*[1] Well known in San Francisco as "Grizzly Adams," he had brought his California Menagerie with him—a collection of huge grizzly bears and other wild animals that he had captured in the western mountains. Now he was heading for Barnum's American Museum on Broadway. He intended to make arrangements with its proprietor, Phineas Taylor Barnum, to show his wild animals in New York.

His gray hair and beard made Adams look much older than his forty-seven years, but his features were clean-cut, his eyes clear and piercing. Years of living in the western mountains had sharpened his senses so that they could see and hear and smell anything of interest in the wild country. That day they were taking in all the sights and sounds of the big city.

New York, with a population of more than eight hundred thousand, was the leading commercial center of the United States. From Castle Garden, the immigration center at the southern tip of Manhattan, to the northern limits of the city at Fiftieth Street, the great metropolis was throbbing with life.

The Hudson and East Rivers were thick with steamers— small ferries as well as snorting side-wheelers that belched smoke from their tall stacks. An occasional clipper ship glided past with white sails spread, as stately as a swan. The docks that fringed both rivers were forests of tall masts and curled canvas.

Horse-drawn carriages and hacks rumbled through the cobbled streets, the drivers shouting at one another and missing collision by inches. On the corners, food vendors sold fruit, meat pies, and flavored soda water. Newsboys hawked the *Herald* or *Tribune*: "Extra, extra! Read all about it! Get your papuh here." Pedestrians scurried about like ants, most of the men in rough working clothes, but a sprinkling of business men in frockcoats and tall stovepipe hats. Many of the women were decked out either in long, rustling dresses or hoopskirts, and wore colorful bonnets or plumes. Just like the women in San Francisco, Adams noted. With

New York City riverfront, 1850s.

the Overland Stage and the new Pony Express, California wasn't behind the times anymore.

Many of the passersby, Adams realized, were stealing curious glances at him as he strode down Broadway. Well, let them stare all they pleased. His ragged buckskin outfit suited him—a dang sight more comfortable than what most of these New Yorkers were wearing.

He finally spotted Barnum's Museum at the corner of Broadway and Ann Street. A huge five-story building with a flat roof bordered with many colorful banners, its sides were

Barnum's American Museum, 1850.

emblazoned with Barnum's name, as well as notices pro-
claiming such sights as "The Fegee Mermaid" and "The Al-
bino Family." Fringing the second story was a wide balcony
where a lively band played minstrel tunes and other popular
pieces off and on all day.

Entering the museum, Adams was quickly ushered into
the proprietor's first floor office. Before him was Barnum
himself. The showman was a large, stout man, faultlessly
dressed, who greeted him with a booming voice. Barnum's
face, fringed with curly hair, featured a bulbous nose, bushy
eyebrows, and a Santa Claus expression. His eyes were kind
and twinkling, but Adams knew that the brain behind them
was calculating and shrewd.

Although the two men seemed to offer a study in con-
trasts, they had several qualities in common. Stories of
Adams's exploits had preceded him to New York, and Barnum immediately recognized the bear trainer as a "character," a surefire attraction in his own right, and even more of
a draw under the skilled promotion which he could provide.
Adams, for his part, knew that it wasn't any accident that
P.T. Barnum was hailed throughout America and Europe as
a premier showman. For twenty years or more he had been
entertaining the public with such stellar attractions as General Tom Thumb, the midget billed as the world's smallest
man; the famous songstress Jenny Lind, the Swedish Night-
ingale; assorted sideshow freaks, including the Siamese
twins, Chang and Eng; and a big traveling menagerie of
wild animals. Barnum was also known as the greatest
"humbugger" of the day, for he delighted in fooling a willing public with such fakes as the "Fegee Mermaid," billed as
authentic, but in reality merely the dried head and torso of a
monkey attached to the body and tail of a fish.

After a few moments of conversation, Barnum told his visitor that he had purchased a half-interest in Adams's California Menagerie just the week before. He had bought it from a man who arrived in town before Adams had, traveling from San Francisco by way of the Isthmus of Panama instead of taking the long, clipper-ship voyage around South America.

Adams protested vigorously. The man had no right to sell half the California Menagerie, he argued. He had merely lent Adams some money, with the animal collections as security for the loan. Barnum pointed out that the man had in his possession a signed bill of sale for half the California Menagerie. Shrugging his shoulders, Adams agreed to accept Barnum's terms as half-owner. "I guess you can do the managing part," he conceded, "and I'll show the animals."

In the course of their conversation, Adams told Barnum that during the past few years he had received hard blows from his "tame" bears on many occasions. Taking off his fur cap, he showed Barnum the top of his head, which, as the startled showman noted, was "literally broken in . . . so that its workings were plainly visible." Barnum remarked that it was indeed a terrible wound, and might prove Grizzly's undoing.

"Yes," Adams agreed, "that will fix me out. It had nearly healed; but old Fremont opened it for me, for the third or fourth time, before I left California, and he did his business so thoroughly, I'm a used-up man. However," he went on in a matter-of-fact voice, "I may live six months or a year yet."

"I'm not the man I was five years ago," he confessed. "Then I felt able to stand the hug of any grizzly living, and was always glad to encounter, single-handed, any sort of animal that presented himself. But I have been beaten to a jelly, torn almost limb from limb, and nearly chewed up and spit out by these treacherous grizzly bears. However, I'm good for a few months yet, and by that time I shall hope to gain enough to make my old woman comfortable, for I have been absent from her for some years."

After watching Grizzly perform with his bears, Barnum wrote that probably no one who saw Adams ". . . suspected that this rough, fierce-looking, powerful demi-savage, as he appeared to be, was suffering intense pain from his broken skull and fevered system, and that nothing kept him from stretching himself on his death-bed but his indomitable and extraordinary will."

Barnum was delighted with the animals Adams had brought from California. There were more than twenty bears in the collection—big grizzly bears, along with some smaller black and cinnamon bears. Biggest of the lot was Samson, a California grizzly promoted as weighing two thousand pounds, but probably topping the scales at closer to twelve hundred. Still, an immense bear. Somewhat smaller was Lady Washington, one of the first grizzlies Adams had captured. The Lady had accompanied him through the western wilds for years, carrying packets on her back and being a handy mountain of furry warmth to sleep beside on cold winter nights. Then there was her son, the fractious General Fremont, who had reopened Adam's old head wound, and Funny Joe, an amiable Rocky Mountain grizzly that Adams had captured as a cub. Among the black bears was one billed as Brigham Young, "the Mormon Screeching Bear," and another called Lola Montez, named by the beautiful dancer while she was in California two years before. There was a huge buffalo bull, an elk, various Indian and wild dogs, and several young mountain lions, as well as a pelican and some vultures. One of the biggest curiosities was an eight-hundred-pound bull sea lion which Adams had captured off San Francisco.

Grizzly had trained a number of the bears to perform special acts. Some danced, others "sang," or turned somersaults. Several were accustomed to being dressed in fancy costumes to play the parts of soldiers or ladies of fashion.

Barnum wondered how Adams had been able to transport such a group of animals successfully from San Francisco to New York by clipper ship, rounding the Horn in some of the wildest seas known to man. Adams readily acknowledged the difficulties he had encountered. In bad weather, the problems of feeding and cleaning the animals were sometimes almost beyond belief. It was during the voyage that General Fremont, in an ugly mood one day, had reopened Adams's old scalp wound. One of the bison had died and as Adams noted, "the fishes, for once, had a novel banquet when we threw his lifeless carcass overboard." Most of the animals, however, had come through in remarkably good shape.

Barnum quickly swung into action as he started making arrangements for showing the California Menagerie and initiating promotion. A vacant lot at Thirteenth Street, between Fourth Avenue and Broadway, was rented for the show, and a large tent erected. An announcement appeared in the April 28 issue of the *New York Clipper,* stating that: "Barnum, of the Museum, and J. M. Nixon, of Niblo's Garden, have entered into a joint engagement with Mr. J. C. Adams, the 'Old Hunter of '49,' for the exhibition of the 'California Menagerie,' which they will open on the 30th ult. at the corner of Thirteenth Street and Fourth Avenue."

As part of the buildup, Barnum arranged to have two pamphlets prepared and printed that set forth Grizzly Adams's life and adventures. He fully realized that Adams "was quite as much of a show as his beasts." Barnum may have written some sections of the pamphlets himself, and

CALIFORNIA MENAGERIE,

EXHIBITED UNDER A COLOSSAL TENT,

AT THE

Corner of Thirteenth street and Fourth avenue,

NEW YORK.

Open from 10 o'clock A. M. till 10 o'clock at Night.

J. C. ADAMS,

Known as "Old Grizzly," the "Wild Yankee Hunter," "Old Adams," &c.,

THE OLD CALIFORNIA TRAPPER OF "'49,"

Has arrived from San Francisco with his wonderful collection of

WILD ANIMALS

OF THE PACIFIC AND THE FAR WEST,

Captured and trained by him during a

PERILOUS HUNTING EXPEDITION

of over four years in

The Rocky Mountains.

A CARD.—The undersigned, grateful for the liberal patronage bestowed upon their respective establishments by the first classes of New York citizens, and strangers visiting the city, and believing that the Tamed Grizzly Bears and other animals, constituting Adams' Great California Menagerie, will prove objects of the greatest curiosity to the public, have made a joint arrangement with Mr. Adams by which they have the entire management and direction of this TRULY NOVEL EXHIBITION. **P. T. BARNUM, Prop. Am. Museum.**
NEW YORK, April 23, 1860. **J. M. NIXON, Prop. Niblo's Garden.**

This is, undoubtedly, the most Curious, Unique, and Interesting

MUSEUM OF ANIMATED NATURE

Ever presented to the Public.

This extraordinary collection of

150 WILD ANIMALS

Includes Ten different species of Bear, among which are : DANCING BEARS, SINGING BEARS, CLIMBING BEARS, BEARS that TURN SUMMERSAULTS, BEARS that have SERVED as PACK-HORSES for Adams, and have slept with him for many years in the Mountains, &c. There are also Bears that are dressed and perform as SOLDIERS ; Bears that appear in LADIES' COSTUME, Hoops, Crinoline, etc. The exhibition also includes hundreds of preserved specimens of Natural History, which have fallen before the deadly rifle of Adams.

First in the order of attraction and novelty is his collection of

TRAINED BEARS,

Some of which are the largest ever put on exhibition in the United States.

Page from short pamphlet published in 1860 to promote the New York showing of the California Menagerie.

Adams certainly wrote or dictated some of the purple prose. Because the grand opening for the California Menagerie was only a few days away, however, Barnum probably hired experienced ghost writers to put most of the story together quickly.

John Adams's experiences in capturing and taming his animals were almost unbelievably colorful and exciting just as they actually happened; when relating them, though, he sometimes couldn't resist adding a few exaggerated touches of his own. He was a good storyteller, and may have embroidered some of his accounts with fanciful details that were not totally true. Although the preface to the longer pamphlet about Adams stated that the story was "written by Himself," and that "I narrate in these pages the truth without exaggeration or embellishment, as I am indifferent to idle notoriety," the many-times-told tales came out quite differently—even when Grizzly was talking about his birth.

Interviewed by one of Barnum's publicity men, Adams declared that he had been born near the Aroostook River in the northern Maine wilderness, ". . . the spot way 'down East' of which it used to be popularly said the inhabitants had the solemn duty to perform for the rest of the American world, in winding up the sun every morning with a windlass. . . .

"I was born under a great pine tree, while my father was felling the timber and building a log hut for the reception of my mother. This, to me, rather important incident (I mean of birth), occurred in the month of May, 1805. My mother was accustomed to allude to that pine tree for many years afterwards; and often she has prophesized of me, as I lay in my crude cradle, playing with my toes, that I would, from the very circumstances of my birth, be in love with a wild

life, and find happiness only away from the haunts and ves-
tiges of civilization."

There is not a word of truth in this picturesque account,
except for the last part of the last sentence. John Adams was,
by nature, truly in love with a wild life; but in plain fact, he
was born on October 22, 1812, in the little town of Medway,
Massachusetts, just twenty miles southwest of the center of
Boston.

2

Shoemaking
and Tiger Training

Medway was a well-settled and rather quiet little town of
less than fifteen hundred people when John Adams, the future bear hunter and trainer, was born. His ancestors had
been among the original settlers, and generations of
Adamses had lived in the area since the 1650s. In 1812, most
of the town's inhabitants were farmers or tradesmen. The
principal industry was shoemaking, which was usually carried on in small home workshops.

Third of eight children, John was the eldest son of Eleazer
and Sybil Adams. Eldest sons usually have plenty of chores
to keep them busy, but John still found time to roam the
surrounding fields and forests during his boyhood, and to
become an expert marksman and woodsman. In love with
the out-of-doors, he dreamed of the day when he would be
able to strike off for himself and live a wild, free life in the
wilderness.[2]

His parents, however, had other plans for him. As soon as

he was old enough, they apprenticed him to a shoemaker. John did as he was told, but rebelled inwardly at being bound to the cobbler's bench, punching holes in the leather with his awl, stitching and shaping the footwear. The fields and forests were where he longed to be.

In the fall of 1833 he celebrated his twenty-first birthday. He was of age at last and was free to do whatever he wanted. Abandoning shoemaking, he contracted with a company of showmen to collect wild animals for them.

The American circus was just getting its start in those days, and every summer wagon shows crawled from village to village throughout the Northeast. The showmen, most of whom were originally Yankee farmers, set up their tents in fields or village greens and put on performances for the curious townfolk and farm families that flocked in from the surrounding countryside. The principal acts of those early circuses were acrobats, tumblers, and equestrians, but a menagerie of wild animals soon became an important part of the show as well. On the road from late spring until fall, the owners customarily took their shows home when winter approached and housed their animals in barns.

About 1820, some of these early circus men leased a building at 36 Bowery in New York City and began to exhibit their animals and acts there throughout the winter. They called their establishment the Zoological Institute, and billed their shows as "educational, entertaining, scientific, and Biblical." Their business thrived. This group of circus men, or one very much like it, hired young Adams to trap animals for them.

For a few glorious months John Adams roamed the forests of Maine, New Hampshire, and Vermont, living as he pleased and glorying in the life of the wilderness. He was successful in his trapping, and captured black bears, mountain lions, bobcats and lynx, wolves and foxes for the showmen. This was the life for him.

The circus men were pleased with John Adams, too. Convinced that he had a unique way with animals, they soon gave him a task that would really test his mettle. Among their collection of animals was a huge and beautiful Bengal tiger, a great attraction in the 1830s, for there were very few tigers in America at that time. This tiger was so ferocious and unruly, however, that nobody could work with it. The circus men asked young Adams to tame and train it.

One of the biggest attractions at the Zoological Institute that year was Isaac Van Amburgh, a young man from Fishkill, New York. Just a year older than John Adams, he had started as an animal keeper for the circus men, and gradually had begun to work with and train lions and tigers. Until then, entering a cage with big cats was unheard of in America; now Van Amburgh was known far and wide as a celebrated trainer. His performance was a sensation. Given a similar chance, John Adams was confident that he could do just as well.

Adams realized that working with a tiger was dangerous, but the prospect didn't faze him. He was supremely confident of his ability—confident to the point of recklessness. He worked successfuly with the great striped cat a number of times. This gave him a feeling of fierce joy, a sense of power over one of nature's deadliest killers. He faced the tiger crouching at the rear of the cage, its ears laid back, lips and teeth bared in a snarl, its long tail slowly switching back and forth. Cautious, he watched every movement the big cat made; the tiger, in turn, followed his every gesture with glowing, amber eyes. It was waiting its chance. One day Adams became overconfident and let his defenses fall for a careless instant. The tiger sprang, striking the man to the floor of the cage. It tore at Adams savagely with its teeth and claws, nearly killing him before his frantic helpers succeeded in dragging him from the cage.

The tiger had mauled Adams so severely about his neck and shoulders that for a time the doctors did not know whether he would live. But John Adams was tough; he had a strong, healthy body and a dauntless will. His recovery was slow and painful, and, as he later observed, "—my constitution was shattered; and for many years my hunting was at an end." At the time, it seemed unlikely that he could ever again undertake any vigorous outdoor work.[3]

His hands were uninjured, however, and he still knew how to make shoes. Refusing to be a burden to his family or anyone else, he went to Boston and took up his old trade. For the next fifteen years he worked as a shoemaker. In 1836, when he was twenty-four years old, he married Cylena Drury of Sturbridge, Massachusetts. Over the next nine years, the couple had three children: Arabella, born in 1839; Arathusa Elizabeth, born in 1843; and Seymour, born in 1845.

John Adams appeared to have become a settled family man, but he still dreamed of that brief period when he had lived the carefree life of a hunter and trapper in the North Woods. Although he had regained his health and strength, those dreams, to all outward appearances, faded further into the background every year. His life had settled into a mold of domesticity, into a treadmill of daily work as a boot- and shoemaker.

Then, in 1848, something happened that shook him out of that mold and radically changed his life. That event was the California Gold Rush.

3

El Dorado,
the Land
of Gold

"The streams are paved with gold—the mountains swell in their golden girdle. It sparkles in the sand of the valleys—it glitters in the coronets of the steep cliffs." That's the way one San Francisco paper in the spring of 1848 trumpeted the exciting news that gold had been discovered on the south fork of the American River, some thirty miles east of what is now Sacramento. With news like that, three-quarters of the men in San Francisco had abandoned their jobs and families by the end of July, and had headed for the beckoning hills.

In the East, the New York *Herald* for August 19 printed the first official news of the exciting discovery. On December 9, President Polk talked about it in his message to Congress: "The accounts of the abundance of gold are of such extraordinary character as would scarcely command belief, were they not corroborated by the authentic reports of officers in the public service!"

That did it. As 1849 dawned, the rush to California began. Thousands of adventurers and goldseekers in the eastern states headed overland for California by way of the Santa Fe Trail, the Oregon Trail, and Mexico. Others traveled by water, sailing around the Horn, or disembarking in Central America to take the short cut across the Isthmus of Panama. Mexicans swarmed northward to the goldfields, and other fortune hunters began to arrive from Canada, Peru, Chile, Europe, and even far-off China. Hundreds of ships from all over the world dropped anchor in San Francisco Bay, spewing out "forty-niners" who hastened off to the diggings as fast as they could go. Almost overnight, San Francisco was transformed from a sleepy little Spanish seaport into a brawling and everchanging gateway to the goldfields.

By the end of the year, more than eighty thousand newcomers had poured into California—three-quarters of them Americans. As they headed for the promised land, their theme song was the popular Stephen Foster melody, "Oh Susanna," which was sweeping the country. They did change a few of the words in the chorus:

> Oh, Susanna
> Oh, don't you cry for me,
> For I'm off to Sacramento with my
> washbowl on my knee.

The news of the gold discovery brought all of John Adams's repressed dreams to the surface. This was the chance of a lifetime, he thought, probably the last big one he would ever get. The Gold Rush seemed to be a heaven-sent opportunity to strike out on a glorious adventure in the western wilderness. In the process, he might even make a fortune for his family.

"It was in 1848 that I caught the gold fever," he recalled.

*Seeking their fortunes, prospectors flocked to the Sierra Nevada in
1849 to search for gold.*

"It afflicted me very severely. No species of stay-at-home advice did me any good whatever. I couldn't get rid of the malady by any other means in the world: so I departed for California."

Adams had worked hard at shoemaking through the years, and had saved his money. He now invested his life savings in a cargo of boots and shoes for the goldseekers. Sturdy footwear, he calculated, was something that every forty-niner would need.

Ill fortune, however, seemed to follow John Adams at crucial moments in his career. His life savings were wiped out in one night when his precious cargo of boots and shoes was destroyed in a great fire on the St. Louis waterfront that burned wharves and warehouses, ships, and stored goods alike.[4]

Although all of John Adams's hopes for the future seemed to float skyward along with the billowing clouds of smoke, he remained, as ever, supremely confident of his own abilities. He still had himself. Undaunted, he struck out for California with a party taking a southern route westward across Mexico. But along the way, Adams's usual bad luck plagued him. In Chihuahua City, Mexico, he fell seriously ill and the group left him behind, presumably to die. Epidemics of cholera were sweeping many parts of the continent at that time, but it is more likely that John Adams was felled by malaria or dysentery. Whatever it was, he was too tough to go under. Recovering, he joined another group that took the Gila River Trail across the burning deserts of southern Arizona—a formidable route littered with wagons and gear abandoned by parched and desperate travelers and the skeletons of both animals and humans. In Los Angeles he fell sick a second time, and again had to remain behind. Again he recovered. Sometime during the fall of 1849 he made his way to Stockton, the last stop before the goldfields.

The year 1849 was the peak of a period of Manifest Destiny, not only for John Adams but for the whole nation. Texas, after gaining its independence from Mexico, had been annexed by the United States in 1845, an act of expansion that triggered war with Mexico the following year. A handful of Americans in California—a Mexican possession at that time—proclaimed an independent "Bear Flag Republic." Two years later, a defeated and resentful Mexico ceded California to the United States, along with the territories of what are now New Mexico, Arizona, Utah, Nevada, and part of Colorado. With the discovery of gold that same year, the sweep westward became an avalanche.

Life in California was wild and unpredictable for the forty-niners, and the first years of the "Bear Flag Republic" were an uproarious, greedy, and lawless time.[5] California

CALIFORNIA REPUBLIC

The present-day California state flag.

entered the Union as a free state in 1850; before that time, however, no federal law was in evidence anywhere. Local vigilante committees were quickly established in various mining settlements, and these took the law into their own hands, dealing out swift hangtown justice to murderers, robbers, and other flagrant disturbers of the peace. It was into this wild atmosphere that John Adams of Massachusetts ventured to stake his claim.

According to his own accounts, he made a fortune three times over during the next three years. At Sonora, the chief mining town of the southern fields, he ran a grocery store and boarding house, among a number of other enterprises. At one time he had valuable mining claims, he avowed, with as many as sixty people working for him at the diggings.

"From the period of my arrival in the country till I went into the mountains," he recalled, "my occupations were various—sometimes mining, sometimes trading, sometimes raising stock and farming. Sometimes I was rich, at other times poor. At one time, in 1850, while farming in the vicinity of Stockton, I possessed thousands of dollars worth of cattle, most of which were stolen from me in a single night. At another time I possessed mining claims which ought to have made me very wealthy; and at another, lands which are now worth many fortunes; but one after another passed out of my hands, partly on account of my own reckless speculations, partly through the villainy of others."

Along with these varied activities, he managed to fit in some hunting and trapping, the favorite pastime of his early days. Now he hunted the biggest and most feared of all western animals—California grizzly bears. Grizzlies were often of enormous size, and had fearsome reputations for killing not only cattle but men. They were a common hazard in the mining areas, as the prospectors soon discovered.

Vaqueros lassoing a grizzly.

Thrill-seeking Spanish cowboys, or *vaqueros,* sometimes captured a grizzly bear by surrounding it on horseback and then lassoing the shaggy beast with pleated rawhide ropes, or *reatas.* If all went as planned, the bear was finally over-powered. Then the victorious hunting party would bind the bear securely with rawhide thongs and carry their victim triumphantly to the nearest town. It would be chained to a post in the center of an enclosed arena and become one of the principal actors in a gory bear-and-bull fight, with crowds of spectators cheering and betting on the outcome. More often than not, the bear won the battle.

Bear-and-bull fights were brutal spectacles. In the rough-and-ready life of the goldfields, however, they were a common and popular entertainment. By 1851, Sonora, the principal town of the southern mines, had a special arena where bear-and-bull contests were staged nearly every Sunday. Some of the bears must have been supplied by Adams.

Frank Marryat, an English author who was traveling in the goldfields, records a glimpse of the Massachusetts bear hunter at this time. Marryat was riding the stage from Stockton to Sonora in September 1851, together with a young Canadian woman with a dog, an "Irish Yankee," and

Frank Marryat drew this illustration of the Sonora stage for his 1855 book, Mountains and Molehills. *He met Grizzly Adams while they were traveling on the same stagecoach.*

two or three miners. "We had, however, one decided character," he reported. "This was a man who, as he gratuitously
informed us, was professionally a bear-hunter, bear-trapper,
and bear-fighter; who, in fact, dealt generally in grizzly
bears. When he shot bears—and it appeared he lived in the
mountains—he sold the meat and cured the skins; but when
he was fortunate enough to trap a fine grizzly alive, a rich
harvest generally awaited him. The grizzly was immediately
transferred, bound hand and foot, to a large and strong
cage; and this being mounted on the bed of a wagon, the animal was dispatched to some large mining town in the vicinity, where notice was given, by means of handbills and
posters, that 'on the Sunday following the famous grizzly
bear "America" would fight a wild bull, etc. etc. Admission,
five dollars.' "

In the matter of catching grizzly bears—or any other
beast, for that matter—John Adams was not to be outdone
by anyone, as he was to prove conclusively during the next
few years. It seemed that the memory of the tiger that had
almost finished his career before it was well-started still
haunted him. He felt the need to prove to the world—and to
himself as well—that he was the master of any animal that
lived.

Good as Adams was at catching bears, however, he was no
match for his human competitors in the struggle for gold
and fortune. In the fall of 1852 he lost most of his property
near Stockton through various speculations and lawsuits. As
he later declared, "The lawyers and the judges, in the course
of certain differences and settlements between us, contrived
to rob me of everything I possessed." Adams became so
enraged by what he considered the injustice of it all that he
got up in court to vent his feelings on the machinations of
lawyers, judges, and other human beings in general. "I

would rather live among savages and wild beasts," he ranted, "than with such a thieving, rascally set of scoundrels as this so-called civilized community."

Promptly putting his words into practice, he hitched up his yoke of decrepit oxen, "who wouldn't rise when they lay down unless I lifted them by the tail," to an old wagon "that wouldn't hold together if I didn't soak it for a week," and left Stockton, heading for the "wildest and most infrequented parts of the Sierra Nevada, resolved thenceforth to make the wilderness my home and wild beasts my companions."

4

Expedition
to Washington Territory

Except for the wagon and oxen, the only worldly goods Adams managed to salvage from his financial reverses were two rifles, a Colt's six-shooter revolver, several bowie knives, and a few tools, blankets, and clothes. That didn't matter. John Adams was used to roughing it; the lighter he traveled, the better he liked it.

Creaking and groaning behind the placid oxen, the wagon slowly made its way eastward through the San Joaquin Valley, past the settlements and mining camps, and upward through the foothills of the Sierra Nevada. The majestic peaks loomed ever higher and nearer. Left behind were the hordes of miners grubbing after gold; left behind were the quarrels and deceits of civilization. Up here the air was fresher, the water cleaner, the rugged landscape still wild and unspoiled. The farther John Adams went, the better he felt.

He gazed with satisfaction on the towering pines and spruces that clung to the steep slopes. In peaceful mountain meadows he glimpsed mule deer browsing. At sight of him they would stop and stare for a moment, their huge ears pricked forward, before bounding away. Vultures circled overhead, and occasionally a huge condor was silhouetted against the bright sky, the flight feathers at the tips of its broad wings spread like outstretched fingers. Coyotes barked, and sometimes he heard wolves howling in the distance. John Adams felt that he had come once more to his real home, the wilderness.

Heading toward the headwaters of the Stanislaus and Tuolumne Rivers, he stopped in a wild and isolated little valley, some fifteen miles northeast of Sonora. Here was plenty of good pasturage for his oxen, and plenty of pure water. All about him was glorious mountain scenery. As far as Adams knew, there were no white men or settlements for many miles. He would make his camp here.

A tribe of California Indians—"Diggers," the prospectors called them—lived nearby.[6] Simple people, they moved up and down the slopes of the mountains with the seasons, living mainly on nuts, acorns, roots, and whatever small game they could take with their snares and bows. Adams made friends of them, and from time to time supplied them with larger animals bagged by his rifles. In return, the grateful Indians helped him to build a log cabin, and to cut and stack some hay for his oxen to eat during the winter.

The Indians also tanned the hides of the deer he gave them, and, before the tribe moved down into the lowlands for the winter, the squaws made him a couple of fringed buckskin suits. These so delighted Adams that thereafter he seldom wore anything else. Like most forty-niners, he had let his beard and hair grow long. He had just turned forty that fall, and was in his prime, but his hair was already turning gray. Dressed in his fringed buckskins and wearing his fur

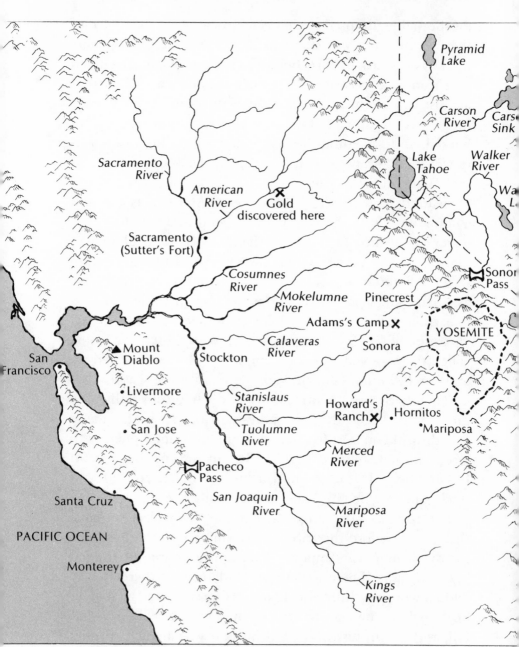

Gold Rush California, scene of many of Grizzly Adams's adventures.

cap, he looked every inch the old mountain man.

Snug in his cabin during that winter of 1852–1853, he gloried in his hermitlike existence, and remembered the time as among the happiest of his life. When his small stock of groceries ran out, he made do with the abundance around him. He pounded the grains of wild grass into flour, and made coffee from roasted acorns. Wild herbs were good for brewing tea. And there were always plenty of animals nearby to keep the stewpot filled.

Although Adams said that he retreated to the mountains "to live in peace, not to levy war upon the natives of the forest," he began once again to take some animals for their skins and hides. Remembering his brief fling at tiger training in New England and capturing grizzly bears in the goldfields, he constructed several log traps with drop doors for catching bears in the Sierra Nevada. Hunting and trapping were in his blood; so was the excitement of matching wits with wild animals—the bigger the better. "I was seized with the insatiable desire," he later confessed, "to make myself master of the untamed, but I believe not untamable, denizens of the mountain range."

In due time he captured several young grizzlies in his traps. "Having subdued them and rendered them comparatively docile and obedient," he took the tamest one down to Mariposa in the spring of 1853 and wrestled it in public. For this performance he received eight hundred dollars. Soon afterward, he took his bears to Stockton and delivered them to two men who agreed, for half the profit, to take them to South America with them and sell them there.[7] The money was welcome, for Adams had that spring purchased the land on which his camp was located.[8] He also had his wife and children back in Massachusetts. They no longer had his income as a shoemaker to keep them going.

As these activities showed, Adams's bitter attitude toward the "civilized community" had softened somewhat during the winter. He had a naturally competitive spirit, and now he was ready once again to take his chances in the world of commercial rivalry and competition. This time, however, he would do it his way. Hunting and trapping were a way of life which he knew and enjoyed, a way of life in which he excelled. It was an occupation in which he might yet gain the fortune that had eluded him at the diggings.

Full of confidence and enthusiasm, he contracted—with whom was never made clear—and received financial backing to collect wild animals of California and adjacent areas. Many of these animals would be shipped to Boston and disposed of there. He immediately started making plans for a summer hunt in Washington and Oregon Territories.

Closing his Sierra campsite, he went south through the foothills to a ranch near Hornitos owned by an acquaintance, William J. Howard.[9] There, he traded his oxen for two mules, and stocked up on provisions and ammunition. At the ranch he met a tall young man by the name of William Sykesey, to whom he took an immediate liking. Sykesey had long black hair and high cheekbones, indicating some Indian blood. He was a seasoned woodsman, had a good rifle, and was a reliable shot. All of these were sterling attributes, in Grizzly's opinion.

Another point in Sykesey's favor was that he had already been to Washington Territory. This northern country had been part of the Oregon Territory until that very spring, when it had been given separate territorial status. Grizzly immediately signed Sykesey on as a companion for the coming hunt.[10]

The two of them headed north to Strawberry Ranch, not far from Adams's winter cabin. There Grizzly hired two Indian youths as helpers for the expedition. In their teens, both boys had lived and worked among whites, and could speak English fairly well. They were good-humored and willing, and knew how to handle guns. Since their Indian names were tongue twisters, Grizzly promptly dubbed the older boy Tuolumne, and the younger Stanislaus, after the nearby rivers of the same name.

It was a beautiful morning in May when the four of them started for Washington Territory, their mules loaded with supplies. They traveled northward along the shoulders of the mountains, the high peaks of the Sierra Nevada to their right, the valley of the Sacramento to their left. After two weeks of travel, they reached the Klamath region of the California-Oregon border. Here they captured their first wild animals—two black bear cubs. Squalling lustily, the two little bears were slung in saddlebags on either side of one of the mules and carried along.

On they went, working their way between the Cascades and Blue Mountains as they pushed into Washington Territory. Beyond the Great Bend of the Columbia River they crossed the Snake or Lewis River, and plunged into the wilderness to the northeast. Somewhere in the wild country of what is now either eastern Idaho or western Montana, they came to a pleasant valley where they established their summer camp.

By now, Adams was eager to get started on some real animal collecting. He explored the countryside tirelessly and before long discovered a grizzly den on a mountain slope not far from camp. Tracks and other signs showed him that the den was occupied. A bit of spying gave him a fleeting glimpse of the bears—a big female grizzly with two yearlings. The cubs, which he judged to be about sixteen months old, were the best-looking young bears Adams had ever seen.

He was determined to capture and train them. But, first, he had to deal with the mother bear.

The three grizzlies, he noted, used the same trail every night as they traveled from their den to the broad valley below to forage. Studying the lay of the land, Grizzly decided to ambush the bears along this path as they returned to their den when they had finished feeding. Before dawn one morning, he concealed himself along the trail and waited, his rifles carefully loaded and ready beside him.

After a considerable wait, he heard snuffling sounds in the distance, and then the soft yelp of a cub. Soon he spotted the trio of bears padding up the trail toward him. When the mother grizzly was close, he fired his Kentucky rifle and hit her in the chest. Snarling with pain, the old bear fell to the ground. Then, spotting Adams, she struggled to her feet and charged directly toward him.

Snatching up his smaller Tennessee rifle, Grizzly fired into her open mouth, and the valiant mother bear dropped in her tracks, the ball lodged in her brain. In a few moments she was dead.

When he was sure she would not get up again, Adams seized his lasso and ran toward the two cubs. Frightened by the sudden action, confused by the fact that their mother lay sprawled and still, they crouched beside her. As Adams approached, however, the two young bears raced away at full speed. They ran until both they and their pursuer were nearly worn out, then suddenly changed their tactics. Wheeling about, they charged straight at their tormentor.

Now, John Adams realized, the shoe was on the other foot. These were only yearlings, but each grizzly had formidable teeth and claws, and weighed about one hundred and fifty pounds. Without time for any other action, he scrambled into the nearest tree to get out of their reach.

Growling and snapping, the two aroused youngsters tried to climb up after him, but Adams pounded at their paws with a stout limb to keep them down. The two bears were so ferocious that Grizzly had to laugh inwardly at his predicament. Here he was, the mighty hunter of great bears, treed by a couple of cubs!

Luckily for John Adams, the young grizzlies quickly tired of their sport and wandered away after a half hour. As soon as he was sure they were gone, Grizzly climbed down from the tree and made his way back to camp. It was clear that he would have to change his tactics if he wanted to capture these cubs. He was determined to have them, for they were beautiful young animals in perfect condition. Besides, he couldn't help but admire their spirit.

5

The Capture
of Lady Washington

Grizzly decided that what he needed to capture the young bears were horses. Mounted, he and his companions could keep pace with the cubs and exhaust them. They didn't have any horses of their own, but the Indians who lived in the area did. There was a sizeable Indian village—Nez Percés, he thought—not far from them.[11] Adams had already met several of the warriors while hunting, and had shared his meat with them. The Indians seemed friendly enough, and they had plenty of horses. Perhaps he could borrow some from them.

Loading a sack of dried venison on one of his mules, Grizzly set off for the Indian village to see what sort of a trade he could make. The leader of the tribe was a good-natured and shrewd old chief named Kennasket. He was pleased to receive the gift of dried meat, and agreed to lend the white hunter three horses for a few days, provided one of his braves went along to see to their safe return. Grizzly readily agreed to these terms. He liked Indians, and had always treated

34

them fairly. Most Indian troubles, in his opinion, were due to white men taking advantage of the Indians in one way or another.

The next morning, Grizzly Adams left the young brave, named Pompey, in camp with Stanislaus while he, Sykesey, and Tuolumne set off with the horses to capture the cubs. His new plan was to surprise the two young bears as they lay by their slain mother—as he was confident they would do— and then to herd them down the trail to the open valley. There he and the others would pursue them on horseback until they were exhausted and easy to capture.

Grizzly stationed his two companions in a clump of bushes and cautioned them not to move until he gave the signal. Then he circled through the chaparral toward the spot where the dead she-bear lay. Sure enough, there were the two cubs huddled beside their mother's carcass, as though trying to draw some accustomed warmth from her cold body. Moved at the sight, Grizzly watched for a few moments. Perhaps he felt a twinge of remorse over having killed the old bear, but he still had to have those two young ones! Careful as he was, the cubs soon spotted him and dashed down the trail toward the valley. Grizzly followed on horseback, confident that his plan was working.

Ahead, his two eager companions jumped the gun. Whooping and hollering, they rode out of concealment too soon and stampeded the two young bears. Instead of continuing down the path, as expected, the cubs dashed into some dense underbrush, where the horses could not follow, and quickly disappeared. They were proving harder to catch than Grizzly had expected.

The next morning, Adams and his companions set out before dawn to try the same plan once again. They soon discovered, however, that the old bear's carcass had been largely devoured since the day before, probably by vultures or wolves. The cubs were nowhere in sight.

Undeterred, Grizzly again changed his tactics. As nearly as he could determine, there was just one spring in the entire valley. It fed a small pond. Sooner or later, the cubs would have to go to the pond to drink. He and his companions would waylay them there.

To test his plan, that evening Grizzly stationed himself at a good vantage point near the pond and waited. The hours passed, and the moon rose pale and clear over the mountains. Visibility was good. It was almost midnight when the cubs came to drink, just as he had figured. Springing to his feet, Grizzly dashed toward them with his lasso twirling overhead. For the third time the cubs escaped, fleeing into the underbrush.

At sundown the next evening, Adams marshalled his companions for still another attempt. He stationed Sykesey and Tuolumne in tall sword grass near the pond, and cautioned them not to show themselves until he gave the signal. He hid himself in the same way, and settled down for another long wait. They would succeed this time—he felt it in his bones.

Several deer and pronghorn antelopes came to the pond to drink, and then a pack of wolves. Nothing else stirred. The stars circled across the night sky and faint streaks of light began to appear in the east before he finally heard grunts and snorts from the nearest slope. The cubs were on their way.

Grizzly watched as the two young bears waded into the water to drink and wallow. After a few moments they climbed ashore and began to wrestle playfully with one another. Giving a loud whistle, the agreed-upon signal, Grizzly spurred his horse forward, his lasso in hand. Sykesey and

Tuolumne dashed from their hiding places, and all three horsemen converged upon the cubs. In the confusion, each cub ran off in a different direction. Shouting to his companions to follow one of the cubs, Grizzly pursued the other as it ran toward the valley.

On his Indian pony, Grizzly kept up easily with the bear. After a chase of about a mile, he made his first attempt to capture it. Swinging his lariat, he saw the rope settle over the cub's head. But before he could draw the noose tight, the bear tossed it off with its paw and a shake of its head. Again and again he cast his noose. Each time the yearling either dodged it or shook it off.

By the time it had run several miles, the young grizzly began to show signs of exhaustion. Grizzly finally saw his noose settle around the quarry's neck and draw tight. Success at last!

He dragged the cub a few feet to knock it off its balance; then, careful to keep the lasso taut, he leaped to the ground as the young bear gasped for breath. Before the yearling realized what was happening, Grizzly had looped a rope muzzle around its jaws and buckskin thongs around its feet. In a moment the grizzly was securely bound and helpless.

Grizzly Adams stood back to admire his prize. The youngster was a female, he noted, in perfect condition. Her fur was thick and brown, and she had the long, straight claws and the dished-in face of the typical grizzly. The cub stared back at him with defiant brown eyes. She snarled, curling her lips and baring her sharp, well-developed teeth. Grizzly grinned appreciatively. She had plenty of spirit, this bear! He decided to name her Lady Washington, for the territory where she was born.

Reluctantly leaving the cub to be carried to camp later, he rode back to the spring to find out what luck Sykesey and

Dime and Half-Dime novels, such as this 1882 issue of Beadle's Boy's Library, *made legend of Grizzly Adams's adventures and exploits.*

Tuolumne had had. When he arrived, he saw that they had been successful too. Beside them lay the other cub, a male, all trussed up. Never in his life had Grizzly seen an animal so securely tied up and wound about with ropes and thongs.

When they saw Grizzly returning empty-handed while they had captured their bear, the two young men couldn't help feeling elated. It wasn't often they could lord it over John Adams. When they taunted him good-naturedly for his failure, Grizzly restrained himself. He didn't mind his partners boasting a bit. Let the boys have their moment of glory. He would have the last laugh.

Sykesey gleefully related how they had pursued the male cub until it had rushed into a grove of chaparral so thick the bear had become entangled. Dismounting, he and Tuolumne had seized the cub with their bare hands and, after a bit of a struggle, had overpowered it and trussed it up. Slinging the young grizzly on a pole, they had carried it to the spring.

After listening to their story, Grizzly asked to see the place where they had captured the cub. He looked it over, then casually remarked that they had an easier place in which to capture their cub than he had for his. In spite of that, he noted, they were all bitten and scratched, while he didn't have a mark on him. Sykesey and Tuolumne glanced at one another, puzzled by this strange talk.

"Look at your hands," Grizzly told them. "Mine are not scratched in that way." He spread his hands to show them. "There's no blood here." With some relish he then related how he had captured the female cub.

Believing that Grizzly was joking, the other two demanded proof. "Have you ever known the old hunter to lie?" Grizzly demanded, drawing himself to his full height and looking them straight in the eye.

Sykesey admitted that he hadn't, and Tuolumne shook his head in agreement. A few tall stories, perhaps, but lies? No. Mollified, Grizzly led them back to where he had left Lady Washington.

The next problem was how to transport the two bears back to camp, several miles distant. Sykesey's idea was to bind each cub on the back of a horse and carry them that way. Grizzly vetoed this idea. Horses didn't like grizzly bears in the best of times, and there was no telling what these Indian ponies would do with live bears lashed across their backs. Tuolumne suggested making a drag of reeds and brush, and pulling the bears back on this crude travois. Adams vetoed that plan too. He had a different idea.

Fastening a stout, buckskin collar around the neck of the male cub, he attached a lariat to either side of it. With a man pulling and hauling on each side, they could walk the cub back to camp, he said. Unfastening the thongs which bound the cub, they tested the plan and found that it worked, after a fashion. The cub followed, but it leaped and struggled so much that both the men and the bear were exhausted by the time they reached camp. Chaining the cub to a tree, Grizzly doused him with cold water to revive him. One cub secured, one more to go.

Pompey had watched the proceedings to this point with great interest. Now the Indian brave told Grizzly that his tribe had a cart which would be just the thing for transporting Lady Washington back to camp—easier on both her and the men. Grizzly agreed to try it out, and Pompey set off with two of the horses to fetch the cart. It was nearly sundown when he returned, accompanied by three other braves who had come along to watch the fun. The horses were pulling one of the strangest-looking vehicles Grizzly had ever seen. It consisted of a tongue and axletree with two solid wooden wheels. Slung between the wheels was a shallow box made of green hides which had dried hard as wood. The horses were harnessed to it with strips of elk hide.

After a great deal of geeing and hawing, Lady Washington, still trussed up, was finally loaded into the cart. The sun had set by this time, and daylight was fading fast. Pompey sprang onto the back of one of the horses and set off for camp at such a rapid clip that the others, on foot, had a hard time keeping up.

By the time they reached camp, it was completely dark. Grizzly chained Lady Washington to a tree, as he had done with her brother. Then, after offering meat and water to both cubs, he sat down with his companions to a hearty meal of black bear steaks prepared by Stanislaus. It had been a very successful day.

Pompey and his friends had such huge appetites that before long the bear steaks were all gone, and some dried venison as well. At last everyone had eaten his fill. Pompey, smacking his lips, suggested that it would be nice if Grizzly got out his leather bottle—his brandy flask. Grizzly protested that the brandy was being saved as medicine.

"Good medicine for red man as well as white," Pompey observed with a grin. After that argument, Grizzly felt obliged to bring out the bottle, and they all toasted their success in catching the grizzly bear cubs. Full of food and drink, they rolled into their blankets in high good humor and went to sleep.

"Such was the manner in which my bear, Lady Washington, one of the companions of my future hunting life, was captured," Adams later told Theodore Hittell, who wrote the story of Grizzly's adventures in 1860. "From that time to this, she has always been with me; and often she has shared my dangers and privations, borne my burdens, and partaken of my meals. The reader may be surprised to hear of a grizzly companion and friend; but Lady Washington has been both to me."

6

Bear
Training

Camp life soon settled into a daily routine which varied little throughout the summer. The camp was close to a spring, with good grass nearby for the horses and mules. There were no buildings or shelters, except for a rough lean-to which served as protection and cookshed when it rained. A fire in the center of a large cleared area burned day and night, both for cooking and to keep wolves and other wild animals at a distance.

Sykesey and the two Indian boys slept with their feet close to the fire. Even in the summer the nights were often chilly in Washington Territory. Grizzly scorned this practice. Wrapped in his blanket, he would bed down some distance away from the fire, his Kentucky rifle always by his side. Back in the shadows, he knew he would be less exposed in case of a night attack on the camp, either by unfriendly Indians or wild animals. If he had to swing into sudden action, he didn't want to be blinded by the glare of the flames.

Grizzly was usually up and about when the first rays of

sunlight showed over the eastern hills, and while the morning star still glowed. After rousing the others so they could begin their morning chores of preparing breakfast and looking after the mules and horses, Grizzly busied himself with watering, feeding, and training his wild pets. He had four bear cubs now: the two little black bears captured on the way to Washington Territory, and the two yearling grizzlies. Before the summer was out, there would be a number of other young animals as well: wolf pups, mule deer and pronghorn antelope fawns, and several gawky elk and buffalo calves.

The two little black bear cubs, captured when they were hardly bigger than housecats, were the camp pets. Lively balls of woolly fur, they quickly became so tame that they were allowed the run of the camp. Grizzly named one of them General Washington, and the other Buchanan, after a crusty old mountain man he had known.

Friendly and playful as puppies, General Washington and Buchanan dogged the men's heels. They made nuisances of themselves in camp, and were continually underfoot while Stanislaus was preparing the meals. They took mischievous delight in stealing whatever they could while his back was turned.

Grizzly Adams was their god. Watchful and curious, they followed him wherever he went. They tried to tag along when he went hunting, and Grizzly learned to steal quietly away while the cubs were snoozing. As soon as they wakened, Stanislaus told him, they would run back and forth looking for their master, crying and sniffling all the while.

As an experiment, Grizzly decided to find out whether the cubs would sleep beside him. Putting a light leash on each, he tied the leashes to a stake, and then made a snug nest for the cubs in his blanket. They were restless at first, and kept Grizzly awake. He tried to quiet them, but without much success. Finally he got up, scolded them roundly, and boxed their ears. After that they curled up quietly in the fold of the blanket, and all three slept quite comfortably for the rest of the night.

Training the two yearling grizzlies was an entirely different matter. Lady Washington and her brother, whom Grizzly had named Jackson, each weighed close to two hundred pounds or more by now.[12] Members of a naturally fiercer species than the black bear cubs, they still acknowledged no master. Grizzly kept them chained to trees at the edge of the camp clearing. Here they paced back and forth, growling at anyone who came close to them.

Grizzly was delighted with the defiant spirit the two yearlings showed. Lady Washington especially appealed to him. She was "cross and perverse," he observed, "as well as inclined to have her own way under all circumstances. . . . I fell in love with the cub because she *was* so ill-natured. I felt a species of delight in subduing, little by little, a will so resolute, a temper so obstinate."

For some days, Lady Washington snapped and growled whenever Grizzly came near her. Lips drawn back in a snarl, she would rush forward, stretching the chain taut as she tried to attack him. Grizzly always watched his step when he approached her. He respected the yearling grizzly's natural weapons—those bone-crushing jaws and teeth, and those two-inch claws that could rip the hide right off one's back.

One day, however, he dropped his guard for a moment, just as he had done years ago with that Bengal tiger. Seizing her opportunity, Lady Washington lunged forward and raked him toward her. Clawing and biting, she attacked him so savagely that in the minute it took him to twist out of her grasp, Grizzly was badly torn and bleeding, but not seriously wounded.

Grim and angry, as much at himself as at the bear, he promptly cut himself a stout tree limb as a weapon. His bloody wounds and the pain he felt had stirred him up and kindled his determination. If necessary, he would tame Lady Washington by brute force, he vowed to himself. He approached her again, wary this time, and careful to keep out of reach of her teeth and claws. It was to be a contest of wills. Using his stout limb, Adams struck repeated blows at the bear. Leaping and snarling, she fought back furiously at both the weapon and the man who wielded it. Wild with anger and frustration, she was soon frothing at the mouth. Sykesey and the two Indian boys begged Grizzly to stop, but Grizzly answered them only when Lady Washington sank panting to the ground, completely exhausted. The grizzly had been dreadfully aroused, he admitted; but so had he! In spite of that, he assured them, he had taken care not to hurt anything more than her pride.

Adams had grown up at a time when "Spare the rod and spoil the child" was the general rule. He had applied that rule to Lady Washington just as, no doubt, it had been applied to him as a boy. As he later acknowledged, "It is beyond question, a cruel spectacle to see a man thus taking an animal and whipping it into subjection; but when a bear has once grown up, untutored, as large as the Lady was, this is the only way to lay the foundation of an education—and the result proved the judiciousness of my course. In a short time afterward I patted her shaggy coat; and she gradually assumed a milder aspect, which satisfied me that she would not soon forget it. As she became calmer, I gave her a greater length of chain; and upon feeding her, she ate kindly and heartily, and gave good promise of what she afterward became—a most faithful and affectionate servant."

From that day on, Lady Washington's disposition improved, and Adams kept his temper in check. He worked patiently with the young grizzly every morning and evening. Within a week he was able to remove her chain and lead her around camp by a lariat attached to her collar. She still occasionally exhibited a stubborn streak, when she would lie down and refuse to be led any farther. Grizzly would then remind her who was master by giving her a couple of light raps on the back. At that, she would get up rather grumpily and follow him once more. She never again tried to attack him.

"It is with bears as it is with children," Adams observed. ". . . although much allowance is to be made for the stock from which they spring, yet, if the right course be taken, their natural characters may be modified and improved to such a degree as to be a subject of wonder."

In some ways, Jackson, the male grizzly cub, posed even more of a training problem than Lady Washington. He fought the leash by rearing back on his haunches and growling defiantly. Whenever Grizzly tugged at the chain, the stubborn young bear would swat at it or seize it in his teeth and shake it. Hair bristling, lips drawn back in a snarl, he would dare Grizzly to tug again.

Day after day, Jackson obstinately refused his instruction at leading, and Grizzly finally decided on drastic measures for him, too. First he fastened one end of a lariat to Jackson's collar, and the other end to the horn of a saddle strapped on the back of one of the mules. Mounting the mule, Adams tugged sharply at the lead. As usual, Jackson sat back on his haunches and braced himself against the pressure. Grizzly gave the mule a "gee-up" and she started off, dragging the surprised bear behind her.

Roaring with indignation, the yearling bear scrambled to his feet and sprang to attack the mule. The supposed victim promptly kicked out with her hind legs and sent the half-grown bear sprawling in the grass. After a few similar treatments, Jackson padded behind meekly enough. Soon he was following the lead as well as the Lady.

Grizzly Adams took pains to praise both Jackson and Lady Washington when they behaved as he wanted. He would pat Jackson on the head and scratch him under the neck. Eventually the bear became as eager as a dog for such attention. Stretching forward, eyes half-closed, he would wait to receive the praise and the friendly pats.

Such eagerness for attention prompted Adams to believe that "the grizzly bear possesses a nature which, if taken in time and carefully improved, may be made the perfection of animal goodness. . . . taken at an early age, his playfulness fostered, accustomed to the sight and sedulous attention of his master, and managed with a firm, but at the same time, gentle hand, he grows up a devoted friend, exhibiting such remarkable qualities of domestication as almost to lead one to suppose that he was intended, as well as the dog, for the companionship of man."

Once his initial obstinacy had been overcome, Jackson revealed a "pleasant countenance," as Adams noted. But Lady Washington was his favorite. She was soon tame enough to follow Grizzly without a leash of any sort. Now he continued her training with lessons in carrying a pack. Filling a fifty-pound flour sack with earth, he gently eased it across her back and tied it firmly in place. The surprised Lady promptly reached back, seized the bag with her teeth, and ripped a hole in it. As the dirt streamed out, Grizzly gave her a good scolding and a few smart raps with his stick. Soon she submitted to the weight on her back without protest.

Although time-consuming, bear training was only part of Grizzly's daily schedule. He and the others continued to hunt and trap as usual. As Lady Washington's education progressed, he began to include her on short trips away from camp. One day he took her with him when he and the others set out to build a new bear trap four miles from camp. Lady Washington was on her best behavior, much to Adams's satisfaction. She followed obediently, and watched patiently while the men cut down trees and constructed a big log trap with drop doors. At lunchtime, she sat beside Grizzly and shared his food.

That evening, as they made ready to return to camp, Grizzly lent Stanislaus his rifle, keeping for himself only his pistol and bowie knife. They needed fresh meat, so the others were going on a short hunt on the way back to camp to try to get some venison.

As he and Lady Washington made their way back, Grizzly spied several deer in a small clearing. Perhaps he could pick up some venison himself, even though he had no rifle. He started a careful stalk through the brush toward the deer, the bear padding along behind him. If he could get close enough, he could drop one of those deer with his pistol.

He was well into a thicket of dense brush, halfway toward the unsuspecting deer, when he came upon some freshly dug earth and a giant paw print. Fresh grizzly bear signs! His scalp prickled as he froze, the Lady huddled beside him. His Colt revolver, as he well realized, was not enough to stop an angry wild grizzly bear.

Adams often took unbelievable chances, but he was seldom foolhardy. It would be wise, he decided, to abandon the deer stalk and make tracks for camp while it was still daylight. Turning about, he began a cautious retreat through the thicket. Behind him, he heard Lady Washington snort, then grind her teeth together in an agitated chatter.

Wheeling around, he saw a huge old male grizzly bear standing on his hind feet just beyond Lady Washington. Motionless, Grizzly stared at the bear, and it stared straight back. The trapper held his breath. This was a big bear. "That it had hostile intentions," he later declared, "all his actions clearly showed, and there I was, almost without arms, and with the Lady as well as myself to take care of." Any sudden movement or noise might make the giant charge. On the other hand, an unexpected noise might make it retreat. A gamble, either way.

Stealthily, Grizzly stretched out his hand and unwound the chain from around Lady Washington's neck, all the while watching the big bear. Lady Washington stood firm beside him, and the wild grizzly was equally motionless, seemingly undecided about what to do next. Unable to endure the suspense any longer, Adams finally made up his mind. Letting out a wild war whoop, he fired his pistol into the air and at the same time rattled Lady Washington's chain.

Startled, the old grizzly snorted, then dropped to all fours and took to his heels. Such unpredictable action was more than he had bargained for!

Whooping repeatedly, Grizzly and the Lady pursued the big bear until he was out of sight. Then they stopped, and Grizzly heaved a sigh of relief. Patting the Lady warmly, he started back to camp as fast as he could go.

"Such was the first instance in which Lady Washington,

Lady Washington and her master confront a wild grizzly.

my faithful friend and constant companion for many years afterwards, stood side by side with me in the hour of danger and dire alarm," Grizzly recalled, ". . . from that time, I felt for her an affection which I have seldom given to any human being."

7

Courage,
Cowardice,
and Comradeship

As the long summer days went by, Grizzly and his companions followed a daily work schedule that kept them busy from dawn until after dark. Following a hearty breakfast, they would set out, the sun barely above the horizon, to start on their main activity of the day. They built several log traps for capturing bears and wolves, and spent many hours hunting. Huge quantities of meat were needed not only for themselves, but also to feed the animals they had captured. The furs and hides they took would add to the profits of the expedition.

Stanislaus usually remained in camp to prepare meals, look after the animals, and perform other routine chores. Tuolumne, a more experienced hunter and marksman, usually accompanied Grizzly and Sykesey on their daily rounds. Sometimes the three worked together, but Grizzly often preferred to hunt alone.

When everyone returned to camp in the evening, the

main meal of the day was eaten. After the wild animals had again been tended, Grizzly and his companions would sit sociably around the campfire and entertain one another with stories of their past adventures and their hopes for the future. Puffing at his pipe, Grizzly would listen to the yarns that Sykesey and the Indian boys related, and tell his own tall tales. The more Grizzly got to know his companions, the better he liked them.

"Upon first entering the mountains of California," he recollected, "I carried all my cares as well as my property with me, taking no thought of others, having only myself and my oxen to provide for. In plain terms, I was a misanthrope. . . . But with a change in my circumstances, my feelings also changed. As my little camp increased, I began to know again that I had duties and obligations to fulfill toward others; . . . I gradually threw aside my indifference, and instead of following entirely the narrow maxim of 'mind your own business,' I gradually learned . . . that one's own business embraces the business of others too."

Grizzly's changed feelings toward his companions did not, however, make him hesitate to give any one of them a tongue-lashing if he thought it was needed. Nor did he hesitate to indulge his sometimes cruel taste for practical jokes.

One day the whole group joined Pompey and several of his Indian friends for a pronghorn antelope hunt. After a successful day, Grizzly and most of the remaining party started back to camp with a load of meat, leaving Tuolumne behind to guard what was left until Grizzly came back for it. Returning with the mules after several hours, Grizzly found Tuolumne fast asleep. Determined to teach the boy a lesson, he quietly loaded the antelope carcasses on the mules and led them off into some concealing brush. Then he took the bearskin which served as a blanket for one of the mules and wrapped himself in it. Crouching in the tall grass near Tuolumne, he let out a bloodcurdling growl.

Startled from his sleep, Tuolumne leapt to his feet and reached for his rifle. Grizzly growled again and rose up. With that, the frightened youth forgot about his rifle. Taking to his heels, he ran away as fast as he could go. Grizzly watched until he had disappeared, then picked up the abandoned rifle and headed back to camp. There he found Tuolumne telling the others a story about a monstrous bear that had attacked him and, indeed, pursued him almost back to camp. Grizzly kept quiet for the moment.

That night, as they made ready to sleep, Grizzly warned Tuolumne to keep a good lookout. "That bear has got a smell of your meat," he cautioned, "and he'll be sure to call on you before morning."

Tuolumne shivered at the thought, and became so agitated that Grizzly finally took pity on him. He told his young helper what had really happened, then reproached him for his cowardice and for sleeping on the job in the first place.

The others laughed when they heard the story, but Tuolumne refused to admit the truth of Grizzly's version, doggedly answering all their sallies by saying that he had to believe what he had seen with his own eyes.

Brave and fearless himself, Grizzly had little patience with any man's show of cowardice, no matter how great the danger. He and Sykesey were building a bear trap one day when they were surprised to see a big female grizzly scrambling down a nearby hill, back end first. The bear was so close to them that Grizzly realized that they were in a critical situation. One wrong move and the bear might charge. Sykesey realized the danger too, and was quite nervous. Reassuring his companion, Grizzly told him to hold his own fire while

Grizzly fired at the big bear. If his shot proved ineffective, then Sykesey was to shoot. In any event, the two of them must stick together to see the danger through.

As the bear came within shooting distance, Grizzly took aim and fired, even though he did not really have a good shot. Sykesey fired his gun a few seconds later, then took to his heels as the bear came tumbling down toward them. Grizzly, with no time to reload, stood his ground. Drawing his bowie knife, he made ready to fight the bear hand to paw. To his amazement, the grizzly took no notice of him but rushed past, blood dripping from her wounds. Reloading his rifle, Grizzly hastened after it, but the bear had already disappeared into a dense stand of brush.

By this time, Sykesey had finally stopped running. Now he rejoined Grizzly, muttering that his gun had gone off prematurely and that he had figured he had to do whatever he could to escape. Grizzly looked at him scornfully.

"It's to be expected that a man will act according to his nature," he replied. "Bravery fronts danger, and repels it; but it is the nature of a coward to run . . ."

Although he was chastened by Grizzly's words, Sykesey was still wary. It was dark by now, and camp was three miles away. Much of the trip would be through chaparral where bears or other large animals might lie in wait. What would they do if another bear disputed their passage, he asked.

"It's as easy to fight a bear in the night as in the daytime," Grizzly replied. "A man has to die but once, and when his time comes, it comes."

Showing a touch of spirit, Sykesey flared back, declaring that Grizzly might fight in the dark if he wanted to, but that he shouldn't expect his help.

"It isn't likely," Grizzly retorted, "that a man will stand

fast at night who will run in the day. But don't be alarmed, you have the choice of staying right where you are."

Sykesey became more alarmed than ever at the thought. Without another word, he followed Grizzly as he headed back to camp, which they reached without further adventure.

The next morning they started back to work on the bear trap. As they passed the place where the grizzly had disappeared, Sykesey ventured the opinion that the bear might have been badly wounded, and might be taken with little trouble. Grizzly replied that if his companion would show a little more courage than he had demonstrated the night before, he was willing to go into the thicket and look for her.

Sykesey flushed. "I'll stand by you to the last drop of my blood," he declared.

They entered the chaparral together. It soon became so thick that they had to advance on their hands and knees. Finally they spied a bear den ahead of them. The big grizzly was lying in the entrance with her head in her paws, as though asleep. Grizzly drew his rifle and "placed a ball at the butt of the bear's ear." The bear did not move; she was already dead. After skinning the grizzly and cutting her up, the two men dragged the quarters and hide out of the thicket and loaded them on the mules for transportation to camp. This episode gave Grizzly and Sykesey better understanding of each other's natures.

Grizzly had another narrow escape from serious injury at this time—the result of one of his occasional lapses in judgment and his failure to take reasonable care. The bear trap he and his companions had been working on was almost finished, and he decided to go hunting to get bait for the trap while the others finished building it. After several hours he spied a small band of elk, one of them a huge bull. Taking careful aim from a distance of about seventy-five yards, he fired his rifle. The big elk fell, and, without waiting to make sure that it was dead, Adams rushed forward to cut its throat with his bowie knife. Just as Grizzly got to it, the bull elk

Stunned by a gunshot wound, a bull elk revives and attacks Grizzly Adams.

scrambled to its feet and lunged toward the man. Rearing, it struck at his shoulders with its forelegs, knocking the knife out of his hand. Trying to escape the flying hoofs, Grizzly pulled out his revolver and pumped bullets into the wounded bull. Stunned by one of them, the elk fell. Grizzly then picked up his knife and killed it.

For several days, Adams was sore and bruised because of his impetuous behavior. He did, however, get some satisfaction for his pains. He got a plentiful supply of bait meat for the finished bear trap, and he was able to furnish his companions with a choice roast of elk meat that evening—as good, he declared, as any porter-house steak.

Red Men
and White

A prickly character in many ways, Grizzly was quick to judge others by the same standards he demanded of himself. However hasty, foolhardy, or cruel he sometimes seemed, he considered himself fair and just in his dealings, however impulsive they might be, with both man and beast. He hunted and killed a great many animals during his lifetime. Yet, in his own way, he loved the creatures of the wild. Once his captive bears had submitted to his authority—and that sometimes took a bit of doing, he occasionally admitted to himself—they became his friends and companions, and he looked after them faithfully.

So with people. The way he looked at it, he had been treated so unfairly by "civilized" white men during his first three years in California, that he now viewed most of them with suspicion. Once he got to know an individual, however, and trusted him, he would stand by him to the death.

As for Indians, he viewed them more kindly than most whites did. Although he felt that they were not "civilized" in

59

the same way whites were, he knew they had the same minds, feelings, and wants. Grizzly realized full well that many white men abused and mistreated Indians, considering them little better than animals.

"Over the whole western country," Grizzly reflected, "it seems to be a rule that the white man can injure the Indian with impunity, and no one steps forward to make him the common cause of mankind; but let the Indian retaliate, and the cry of 'Indian depredations' is raised."

Adams himself never had any serious problems with Indians. He treated them honorably, man to man, and they responded in like manner.

Pompey and his friends had proven so helpful in the capture of Lady Washington and Jackson that Grizzly thought it would be a good idea to further cement relations with his Indian allies and neighbors by paying them a visit. A few days after the capture of the two grizzly cubs earlier that summer, he and Tuolumne had set off for Pompey's village, their two mules carrying a goodwill offering of meat.

Knowing how fond the Indians usually were of ceremonies, Grizzly had sent his companion ahead waving a white cloth—a flag to announce their peaceful intent—as they approached the village. After a few moments Tuolumne returned, beckoning Grizzly to come to Chief Kennasket's lodge.

Arriving at the entrance, Grizzly delivered the loads of meat to the chief's wives. The old potentate watched with satisfaction as the gifts were unloaded, and remarked that Gray Beard, as he called Grizzly, was always welcome at his lodge. He was so moved that he volunteered to loan him his horses again.

Grizzly replied that the Old Hunter always kept his promises, and that he hoped the chief would never find cause to complain. With that, the two began to compliment one another on their respective good qualities for a half hour or more.

At last Grizzly decided that he had done all he could as a goodwill ambassador for one day, and made a move to leave. The Indian leader stopped him, however, saying that he wanted to give the white man a present in memory of Kennasket, the great chief. He hoped Adams would keep it as long as he lived.

"The great chief's present will be sacred," Grizzly replied. Kennasket went out to get his gift, and Grizzly wondered what it might be. A sacred headdress? A bearclaw necklace? A wampum belt or some other example of Indian fancy work? He was somewhat surprised when the Indian returned with a tiny black puppy in his arms. Kneeling before Grizzly with this offering, the chief muttered a few inaudible words to heaven, and presented the dog as a great treasure.

Grizzly accepted the puppy gravely. Kneeling, he thanked the chief for this splendid gift and placed it inside his hunting jacket, vowing to treasure and care for it. Then he and Tuolumne started back to camp. Thus ended their first ceremonial contact with the Indians.

Grizzly kept his promise to Kennasket, and the little black dog went to New York with him in 1860.

During the next several weeks, Grizzly and his companions hunted and trapped daily. They captured a number of other animals, among them several wolves, and killed a grizzly bear which, they estimated, weighed a thousand pounds. Soon choice cuts of bear meat were hung on the green boughs about camp, "like choice cuts in a market stall at Christmas," Grizzly reflected.

One morning at dawn, Adams was awakened by an In-

Chief Kennasket of the Nez Percé gives a puppy to Adams as a token of his regard.

dian yell. He watched as his friend Pompey came riding into camp with two other braves. They had come to invite Grizzly and his companions to a great Indian feast and celebration that was to take place in two days. Chief Kennasket, Pompey added, would be very pleased if the great White

Hunter would bring along as much game as possible for the occasion.

Such an invitation was virtually a command, as Grizzly well knew. He replied that he would be most happy to comply, if Pompey and his friends would help with the hunt. They agreed, and for the next two days the Indians and whites scoured the countryside for game, Grizzly leading one hunting party and Sykesey another. On the first day, a bear, several deer, an antelope, and a number of smaller animals were bagged. On the second day, the Indians who had accompanied Grizzly captured two mule deer fawns for his growing menagerie. The trapper was delighted, and told them what good hunters they were. "You excel the White Hunter," he exclaimed. The Indians, although they were flattered by this praise, disagreed. "The White Hunter is a hunter of bears!" they replied.

Loaded down with meat and other booty, Grizzly and his hunting party advanced toward the Indian village. When they arrived, the day before the ceremony, one of Chief Kennasket's wives appoached with a wreath of wild flowers which she placed ceremoniously upon Grizzly's head. Then she escorted him into the old potentate's lodge, where a number of chiefs were already gathered.

Chief Kennasket made a flowery speech of welcome, calling Grizzly his friend and brother. Then Grizzly knelt while the chiefs made a circle about him and placed their hands on his head. They danced and sang around him, repeating the chief's words: "Good is the White Hunter, who comes with much game from the east. No thief is he, but friend and brother of the Red Man. He is welcome."

Not long afterward, Sykesey and the other hunting party arrived, and the same sort of ceremony was performed. Sykesey appeared quite nervous when a squaw placed a wreath on his head, and Grizzly realized that he was alarmed about what might happen next. Sykesey knew very little of the Indians' love of ceremony. He may have thought he was being prepared for slaughter, like a sacrificial lamb. Grizzly told him to kneel, but Sykesey protested; he had never done so in his life, he said.

"But you can surely kneel to say your prayers," Grizzly exclaimed, playing another of his jokes on his companion. Sykesey glanced about wildly, searching for some means of escape. Grizzly's remark made him think that he was going to be killed.

"Pluck up your courage," Grizzly taunted, "and die like a man." Pale as a ghost, Sykesey sank to his knees. The ceremony ended at last, and the man realized that he wouldn't be killed. It was some time, however, before he recovered from his fright.

Kennasket was very happy with all the meat that Grizzly and his companions had brought, and invited them to amuse themselves in the camp. "This night you shall sleep in my lodge," he promised Grizzly. "The White Hunter never sleeps under cover," Grizzly replied, "nor ever where women sleep." Kennasket laughed, and said that his women wouldn't hurt anyone, but that his friend the White Hunter should sleep wherever he wished.

The big evening meal was served in two huge bowls. Grizzly later recalled that the bowls contained a kind of mush made by mixing grass seed, meal, and water in the tureen and then throwing in hot stones till it was cooked. The Indians scooped up this mixture with their fingers and sucked it down with loud smacking noises. Grizzly, somewhat more fastidious, confined himself to eating roasted meat, great piles of which were heaped upon flat stones.

After the feast, Grizzly borrowed a horse and rode back to

his own camp to check on his animals and attend to their needs. By the time he had finished feeding and taking care of them, it was so late that he rolled up in his blanket and slept there.

Up before dawn, as usual, he fed the animals and then rode back to the Indian village, arriving at daybreak. Everyone was still asleep. Grizzly decided to usher in the day and rouse the Indians with a little sport. Spurring his horse to a full gallop, he rode through the village shrieking with all his might, *"Chawawi! Chawawi!"* That cry, as he knew, was an Indian call of alarm over a surprise attack.

Indians rushed out of every lodge greatly frightened, rubbing the sleep from their eyes. As they collected around him, Grizzly assured them that they need not be alarmed. This was just his way of announcing his arrival, he said. His heart was merry. Luckily, the Indians had a sense of humor, too. They laughed heartily as they scattered to begin their preparations for the coming celebration.

There were about fifty lodges in Kennasket's village, with perhaps four hundred people living in them. On the day of the celebration, however, there was an almost equal number of visitors from other villages. As he wandered about the camp, Grizzly saw a few scalps hanging in some of the lodges; none of them, he was assured, had been taken from white men.

Grizzly aroused his companions, who had still been asleep when he arrived. Soon afterward, the chief invited him to accompany him while he examined the area where the celebration was to be held. They walked to a level, grassy spot, with here and there a few spreading oak trees that promised welcome shade. After retiring to the chief's lodge for breakfast, they returned to the meadow. The Indians had cleared the ground of rocks and limbs by this time, and had staked out four or five circles about the size of circus rings, evidently for dancing. Barbecue fires had been started. Soon the crowds began to gather. All of the adult Indians were in their best finery—feathered headdresses, beads, furs, necklaces, and brightly colored shawls. They had decorated themselves with black, vermilion, and other colored paints. Soon the rhythmic beating of drums and a kind of singsong chant from a group of the performers began to roll across the meadow.

At a signal from the chief, the main feast began in midafternoon. The amount of food laid out was prodigious. There were vast quantities of mush and meat—venison, antelope, bear, and smaller game. All in all, Grizzly estimated that there were about two hundred roasts of assorted sizes and shapes. He watched in disbelief at the show of appetites: ". . . such a destruction of food as then took place was astonishing to all my ideas of human capacity." The Indians laughed and joked while they ate, and the young men shouted and whooped in high spirits. They could hardly wait for the activities to come.

Suddenly Chief Kennasket jumped to his feet. Ordering silence, he began a speech, telling the people about the great deeds he had performed in years past, the glory of the tribe, and how this Indian nation was the greatest of them all. When he finished, other chiefs took up the refrain in turn. Finally, the young warriors assembled for dancing. Each held a war club, and the dance took the form of a simulated battle. Time and again Grizzly thought that a brave would be brained, but the club always missed by a hair. Other dances followed, the women taking part in some.

After the dancing, the warriors held contests in archery and other skills. As dusk approached, large fires were built, and the assembled Indians began to dance once again. Grizzly watched them with lively interest. "The forms of the plumed and painted Indians, as they passed to and fro in the ruddy glare of the night fires; the dark shadows and the flickering lights on every side . . ." presented a spectacle that he would always remember.

The celebration continued for most of the night, but Grizzly and his companions left about midnight and headed back to their own camp. After tending their animals, they turned in and slept. Tomorrow they had to get back to work.

9

Death
of a Hunter

One summer evening when Grizzly arrived back at camp after a long day of hunting, his companions greeted him with disturbing news. No one had remained in camp that day, and when Sykesey and the two Indian youths had returned, they saw that the fire was burning brightly, indicating recent visitors. Part of their stores of pepper, salt, and dried meat was gone, and some gun powder as well. Worst of all, the two little black bear cubs—General Washington and Buchanan—had also disappeared.

Grizzly frowned at the news. The nearby Indians were his friends, and he was confident they wouldn't do such a thing. There was nothing unusual about white hunters going into a camp such as his and "borrowing" a few vitally needed supplies, but he wasn't aware of any other white hunters within many miles of them. And why had the black bear cubs been taken? He determined never to leave the camp unguarded again, and directed Stanislaus to remain behind the next

68

day while he and the others continued their hunting activities.

The next morning, Grizzly was awakened by the shouts of Indians. Instantly alert, he recognized Pompey and the other two braves who had helped capture Lady Washington and Jackson. After greeting Grizzly, Pompey told him that Chief Kennasket had agreed to trade him two horses, as Grizzly had previously requested, provided Kennasket got what he wanted in return. Delighted, Grizzly said that he would go over the following day to settle the business. He invited the Indians to breakfast and, while they ate, his visitors told him that a party of white men was camped a few miles away, on the other side of their village.

"They have two black bear cubs just like yours," one of the braves added.

"If they are just like mine," said Grizzly, "they must be mine." He told them how his cubs had disappeared from camp. He was determined to track down and confront these itchy-fingered strangers.

When the Indians had gone, Grizzly, Sykesey, and Tuolumne proceeded on their trapping and hunting rounds, leaving Stanislaus in camp, as before. During the day, much to Grizzly's surprise, they sighted a few buffalo, which were seldom seen west of the Rockies.[13] They pursued them, and Sykesey killed a cow. Over juicy buffalo steaks that evening, Stanislaus told Grizzly that a white man had visited camp while the others were gone. The stranger had told the Indian boy that he was a hunter from Texas, an old friend of Grizzly's.

Grizzly could not imagine who it could be. The report made him more determined than ever to track down these mysterious strangers and find out what they were up to.

Early the next morning, he loaded a mule with two sacks of buffalo meat, and set off to visit Kennasket, as promised. He took along two of the wolf pups which had taken the chief's fancy. The old sachem's eyes lit up when he saw the two woolly pups—"lobos," as he called them. After much talk, he and Grizzly struck a bargain: two horses in exchange for the two young wolves, a black bear cub, two sacks of dried venison, and the buffalo meat. The chief readily agreed to Grizzly's taking the horses with him; the promised bear cub could wait until the hunter had recovered his stolen cubs or captured another one.

After receiving directions from the Indians, Grizzly and Tuolumne set off to find the other white hunters. These turned out to be three Texans, one of whom Grizzly immediately recognized as John Kimball, a companion on the 1849 trip through the Arizona deserts that surrounded the Gila and Colorado rivers. Kimball hailed him enthusiastically, and Grizzly asked what had brought him to Washington Territory.

"Well, to tell the truth, Mr. Adams," Kimball replied, "I never would have got so far, had it not been for that canteen of water which you gave me in the Colorado Desert." He then introduced his two companions as Partridge and William Foster, and the four of them swapped stories about their past adventures. Kimball repeatedly maintained that Grizzly, in his opinion, had saved his life by sharing his canteen with him while they were crossing the desert.

The Texan laughed heartily at the recollection. "One favor deserves another!" he declared. He went on to relate how he had visited Grizzly's present camp several times, but had never found him at home. Finally he had taken a few stores and the two bear cubs, figuring that Adams would hunt them down. That was one sure way of meeting up with him, he said.

Grizzly found it hard to see the sense of arranging a meeting in this way, or, for that matter, how such action could be considered a good turn. How had Kimball known that the camp was Grizzly's, in the first place? But he let these thoughts pass. After the hunters had swapped stories for half the night, they all turned in for sleep.

In the morning, Grizzly and Tuolumne headed back to camp, taking the two bear cubs with them. On the way, they stopped to see Kennasket. The chief was so taken with both little black bears that he traded Grizzly an extra horse for the second cub.

A few days later, the three Texans paid a return visit to Grizzly and his companions, and the two parties decided to join forces for an elk hunt. One evening, after supper, Kimball related how he had been in Portland, Oregon, earlier that summer. He'd seen a ship at the docks that was scheduled to sail for Boston in September. Hearing this, Adams decided that it would be better to take his animals and skins to Portland for shipment to Boston than to take them all the way back to California. The two groups of hunters agreed to hunt and trap together for the next month, and then to start for Portland.

Grizzly thought that the group should capture as many wild animals as possible before heading for Oregon, and take plenty of hides and skins as well. The more they had to trade and sell, the more profit there would be for them. A great deal of dried meat would be needed, too, as food for the bears, wolves, and other meat-eaters during the trip to the coast and on the long ocean voyage.

Grizzly assumed the leadership of the combined parties as a natural right. It was he who decided that some of the group should go on an extended buffalo hunt in a valley some forty miles to the east. Accompanied by Kimball, Foster, and Tuolumne, he set out, leaving the others to hunt and trap from the base camp. After a long day's travel, they reached a beautiful valley that overlooked gently rolling plains. They camped there for the night, and the next morning saw distant, dark objects on the plains—buffalo, the quarry they were seeking.

For several days they hunted the huge, shaggy beasts with great success. On the third day, however, a near-tragedy occurred. They were attempting to drive a small band of buffalo into a marsh, where the big, humped animals would become mired in the soft mud and muck, and could be killed easily. But the band turned unexpectedly and thundered toward Foster, who was stationed to one side.

Foster, as Grizzly had already learned, was an inexperienced hunter who was ". . . anxious to distinguish himself, but yet knew little of that prudence and caution which characterize the true hunter." Grizzly watched in horror as the wild cattle stampeded toward his hunting companion, who had positioned himself and his horse in clear view in front of them, and was waving and shouting in a vain attempt to make them swerve back in the desired direction.

The buffalo kept coming straight at Foster. The unfortunate hunter and his horse disappeared beneath their feet. After the wild cattle had passed, Grizzly galloped up, expecting to find only Foster's trampled remains.

Much to his surprise, he found Foster badly bruised and shaken up, but not seriously hurt. Grizzly promptly made him submit to the cold water cure, his favorite remedy for wounds and bruises. He soaked strips of blanket in cold water and wound them around Foster's bruised body, from the armpits to the hips. The bandages were kept wet, and after several days Foster felt almost as fit as ever.

Soon after Foster's mishap, Grizzly himself had a narrow escape—one that showed, as the incident with the bull elk, that he did not always exercise prudence and caution himself. He and his companions had pursued a band of buffalo into the marsh, where a number of them became mired in the soft mud. After shooting four buffalo, they spotted another, a great bull, mired a short distance ahead. Grizzly hadn't as yet reloaded his rifle; foolishly, he decided to kill the beast with his bowie knife. As he was about to plunge his weapon into the buffalo's neck, it gave a mighty heave, lunging against him and knocking him sprawling. Towering over him, it put its mighty head down on Adams's chest and pushed with its short, curved horns. Grizzly thought his last moment had come.

The soft mud proved to be his salvation, for his body sank. But now the danger was of either drowning or suffocating. Just as he seemed about to disappear beneath the muck, Kimball hastened up and fired his gun at the bull. At the impact of the bullet, the buffalo threw up its head, and Grizzly struggled to his feet. Knife still in hand, he stabbed the beast to the heart and killed it.

After an eight-day hunt, the party headed back to their main camp, loaded down with huge quantities of buffalo, deer, and antelope meat, and the skins of several foxes they had taken. The other group had been equally successful. They had taken and dried a large quantity of meat, and had captured two black bear cubs and three wolf pups, as well.

The night after their return, they were wakened by a griz-

An aroused bison attempts to gore Grizzly Adams.

zly bear that had been attracted by fresh elk meat hung
from trees around the camp. Jumping from his blanket,
Grizzly fired his rifle, and the bear made off with a startled
growl. Foster was beside himself with excitement and immediately wanted to take off after the bear. Grizzly told him it
would be madness to follow such a dangerous animal in the

darkness. Still, he had a hard time curbing the other's enthusiasm. Foster had never killed a grizzly bear, and was eager to do so.

The next morning, Grizzly and his companions had been on the hunting trail for less than an hour when they sighted a large grizzly bear with a couple of yearling cubs. Foster could scarcely contain himself; left to his own devices, he would have fired at the old bear at once. Again, Adams urged caution. He proposed that they approach the bears from a wooded knoll on the other side of the animals. Foster was so intent on an immediate shot, however, that Grizzly reluctantly agreed, exacting only the promise that Foster would not fire until the others had worked their way around to the knoll. Grizzly realized that the young hunter probably thought he could kill a grizzly bear as easily as a buck mule deer. He was soon to learn the difference.

Grizzly and the others were just climbing the knoll when they heard the sound of a shot, followed by an angry roar— the roar of a charging grizzly. Hastening to the top of the ridge, Adams was just in time to see Foster making for a small tree, with the big grizzly in hot pursuit.

For a moment it looked as though Foster would make it. He jumped at the tree trunk and scrambled desperately to climb up into the branches. Close behind him, the bear seized him by one foot before he could swing it out of reach. Tugging, she brought the man crashing down. In a moment she was on top of him, mauling and biting.

Unsheathing his knife, Grizzly ran forward as fast as he could go with the idea of trying to divert the bear's attention from her victim. Time and again he had cautioned Foster and his companions to "play dead" in such dire straits, neither moving nor uttering any sounds, however bitten they might be. Chances were the bear would sniff at its victim and go away. Foster, however, was screaming and struggling. As Grizzly watched, the angry grizzly ripped him open with one sweep of her paw and killed him on the spot. After a moment the half-grown cubs joined their mother and began to maul poor Foster's remains.

From behind a nearby tree, Grizzly took careful aim and fired at the old she-bear. The ball entered her back behind the shoulder, and she fell. She soon got up, however, and charged toward Grizzly. He then fired a second shot which killed her. He reloaded as quickly as he could while his companions rushed toward him. All of them began to shoot at the yearling cubs, which by now were aroused and snarling ferociously.

One of them fell; the other, though wounded, charged Tuolumne and struck him to the ground. Grizzly and Kimball leaped forward and, from opposite sides, plunged their blades into the yearling bear. It sank to the ground and died. Tuolumne was scratched and bleeding, but not seriously injured.

The danger over, Grizzly sent Partridge and Sykesey back to camp for a pick and shovel, so they could dig a grave for their dead companion. While they were gone, he and Kimball prepared the pitifully mauled body as best they could, then settled down to guard the remains until the others returned with the tools. They had a long vigil, since Partridge and Sykesey, for some unexplained reason, did not come back until the next evening.

The following morning they dug a five-foot-deep grave under an oak tree. Finished, they stood in attention before the open grave. Before lowering the body into its final resting place, Grizzly asked Kimball to offer a prayer for Foster. God, the Great Being, was present here in the wilderness,

Adams believed, just as surely as he was in any man-made church. God would hear what Kimball had to say.

His companion agreed, and though he was no more a formal churchman than Adams was, he uttered a moving, if untutored, appeal to heaven to witness these last rites for the dead, and take his faithful servant, William Foster, to his eternal home.

Grizzly said a fervent amen. The hunters then lowered the blanket-wrapped body of their comrade into the grave. Placing branches and leaves over it, they filled the open grave with earth, heaping it into a small mound. A smoothed wooden marker was placed at the head of the grave, and upon the oak tree they carved the name of William Foster, together with the date and the manner of his death. Their sad task finished, they headed back to camp.

"Poor Foster," Grizzly thought to himself. "He was brave-hearted and willing-handed. But he was unfortunate. We had all begun to love him, and may he rest peacefully in the lonely grave to which our rough but friendly hands consigned him!"[14]

10

The Journey to Portland

Grizzly and his companions worked feverishly over the next several weeks, hunting, curing the meat of the animals they killed, preparing skins and hides, and getting their supplies and equipment in shape. They continued to trap animals, too, and by the end of the summer they had a sizeable menagerie of live animals, many of them captured since Foster's death. There were two black bear cubs, a brown bear and her cub, and two young grizzlies. Other meat-eaters included two panthers, two black wolves, two white ones, four black foxes, and several of those large forest weasels called fishers. The hoofed stock consisted of mule deer and pronghorn antelope fawns, and several elk calves.

Autumn was approaching, and the time was drawing near when they had to leave for Portland, if Grizzly was to get back to his camp in the Sierra Nevada mountains before snow fell. Taking a day off from camp activities, he set off to see his friend, Chief Kennasket, to bargain for the horses and men he would need to help transport his supplies and animals to Portland.

Grizzly told the chief what he needed, and said that he proposed to make the transaction a great bargain for Kennasket. The old chief smiled wryly and held up his arm, which was bandaged from wrist to elbow.

"White man very good!" he exclaimed. "But the white man's bargains—very bad!" He went on to explain that one of the black bear cubs that Grizzly had traded to him had bitten him.

"If those bears are so bad," Grizzly replied, "I'll buy them back from you." Kennasket then asked whether he would get back the horses he had traded for the cubs. Grizzly quickly changed the subject. He needed all the horses he could get.

After a lengthy bargaining session, the chief agreed to loan Grizzly thirty horses and six men for the three hundred mile trip to Portland. In return, he was to get two sacks of dried meat for every horse, and six mule deer fawns and one young elk in return for the services of the men.

Bargaining finished, Grizzly and his companions made a last hunt to get as much meat as possible, not only for the trip, but to pay Kennasket as well. After the dried meat and young deer and elk were delivered to the chief, the thirty horses and six Indian braves came to camp, as agreed. Now final preparations began. Saddles for the horses were made by fastening together bows made of green limbs with wooden pins and a few nails, and covering these frames with elk skin. All of the stores were prepared in packs, each marked and numbered. Soon the camp, as Grizzly remarked, "resembled a sort of bazaar, where the packages of a caravan are displayed."

At last everything was ready for departure. At dawn the next morning the horses were packed, and all the wild animals of the menagerie were fed and watered. About noon, camp was struck, and the caravan got underway. And what a strange parade it was!

Adams later described the caravan: "In the first place there were five horses packed with buffalo robes, of which we had about thirty-five; next, four horses packed with bear skins, and several large bear skulls; then, two packed with deer skins; two with antelope skins; one with fox and other small skins; seven with dried meat for the use of the animals on the journey, and, in part, on their intended voyage; one with boxes containing the young bear cubs last caught; two with boxes containing wolves, untamed; a mule with foxes and fishers in baskets; and a mule with tools, blankets, and camp luggage. Almost all the horses, besides the seven specially devoted to the purpose, carried more or less dried meat—even those we rode. But the most remarkable portion of the train consisted of the animals which we drove along in a small herd; these were six bears, four wolves, four deer, four antelopes, two elks, and the Indian dog.

"In the disposition of the caravan, two Indians, who served as guides, rode foremost; next followed the packed horses, with four Indians to attend and govern them; and next myself, with the animals. Kimball, Partridge, Sykesey, Tuolumne, and Stanislaus brought up the rear."

That first day they made it only to Kennasket's village, where they spent the night. Grizzly had one last palaver with the old chief, and Kennasket told Grizzly he wanted to trade back the two black bear cubs. He had lost his enthusiasm for them ever since one had bitten him so badly. Grizzly readily agreed to take them back, and gave Kennasket two sacks of dried meat and four wolf skins in exchange for them.

In addition, he gave the chief one of the white wolves as a farewell present. Kennasket was very pleased.

The next morning, Kennasket invoked the blessings of heaven upon the caravan and asked the Great Spirit to look after them well. Then they started off once again, with almost every man, woman, and child in the village watching their departure. They traveled about twenty miles that day, and then camped for the night, arranging their packs and supplies in a defensive circle against possible attacks by wild beasts or strange Indians. After the animals and men had all been fed, the camp settled down to sleep, with two men stationed as guards.

From that time on they traveled in easy stages, laying over for a day or two when animals or men became weary.

About ten days after they had started, they were confronted by a sudden crisis as they made their way through a narrow valley. A band of fifteen or twenty horses came galloping toward them at full speed. A stampede through the caravan would cause untold damage! Grizzly dashed forward on his horse, swinging his lariat and whooping at the top of his lungs. At the last moment the horses swerved to the right and thundered past, followed by three mounted Indians.

Upon Grizzly's halloo, the three strangers stopped for a moment, and Grizzly learned from them that there was a large Indian village or *rancherio* some twenty-five miles ahead. He impressed upon the three braves that his party was part of a great nation of white people, and that they were bound for the settlements at Portland. He added that the whites would treat the Indians well if they allowed them to pass undisturbed. The Indians agreed, and rode off after Grizzly had given each of them a present of meat.

Knowing that the Indian village was ahead, Grizzly immediately altered course to avoid it. He suspected that if the Indians spotted the caravan, they would demand more tribute and presents than he could afford to give them. For the next several days the caravan made its way through rugged hill country, and finally reached the valley of the upper Columbia River.

Encamped upon the banks of the river, Grizzly looked out over it, trying to figure how best to cross. At this point the Columbia was a wide and mighty river, with a strong current. Grizzly decided that there was just one sure way to test its hazards. Throwing off his coat, he seized a long pole, mounted his horse, and plunged down the bank into the water. Almost immediately the horse was beyond its depth and swimming. In the middle of the river, Grizzly couldn't touch bottom with his pole. When he reached the other side, he rode along the bank for several miles, searching for a better place to cross, but without any success. Plunging once more into the deep waters, he recrossed and returned to camp. He knew that they must build a raft to transport their animals and stores.

The next day he and his companions set to work building a big pine log raft, about twenty feet long and ten feet wide. Over this they installed a rough flooring of split cedar planks. With the raft finished to his satisfaction, Grizzly decided that they would make the crossing the next morning. Late that afternoon, however, several strange Indians blundered into camp. As soon as they had gone, Grizzly decided on an immediate night crossing in order to get away before the whole tribe arrived. The Indians would completely surround them, he was sure, gawking and demanding tribute.

Leaving the loading of the raft to the others, Grizzly tied a number of lariats together. Fastening one end of the long line to a tree on the bank, he plunged into the river on his horse. Crossing, he tied the raft guideline to a tree on the other side. When he returned, he ordered the passage to begin at once.

Dusk had already fallen when the heavily loaded raft was pushed out on its first trip across the river. Eight men pulled at the sweeps and attended the rope guideline which kept them from being swept downstream by the swift current. Grizzly himself stood at the front of the raft. For the first time in his life he was the captain of a vessel of sorts. Although there were some anxious moments, the raft reached the other side without mishap. After unloading, the crew quickly returned and brought over a second load. Then they went back for the third one, which would include most of the wild animals.

Dawn was just beginning to break when all of the animals were finally loaded aboard the raft in groups, and quieted. When they shoved off, Grizzly left his captain's position at the front of the raft and went back to stand among the bears, to soothe them and keep them quiet. All of them, even Lady Washington, were restless in these watery and unfamiliar surroundings. The raft was about two-thirds of the way across the river when disaster struck. The guideline snapped, and the strange Noah's ark was swept downstream. Confusion increased among the animals. Lady Washington and a black bear cub plunged overboard and struck out on their own, following the drifting raft. Stroking desperately with their sweeps, the crew finally brought the raft to the opposite shore without further loss, about a quarter of a mile below the scheduled landing place.

After rounding up Lady Washington and the black bear cub, Grizzly began the job of assembling the animals and supplies. Everything was across the river now except the horses, which would have been the last raft load. Grizzly saw that the Indians were already beginning to gather in large numbers on the far bank, and decided that another raft trip would not be sensible. His only alternative was to swim the horses across. Plunging into the current once again, he crossed to the other side; there wasn't a moment to be lost. Together with Tuolumne and several of Kennasket's braves who had been left to guard the mounts, they herded the horses into the river and across to the opposite shore.

All the men and animals were now collected together in one place, where they camped and rested for the remainder of the day. Early the next morning they continued their journey, traveling southwest by easy stages until they climbed a hill from which they could see the snowy peaks of Mount Rainier and Mount Saint Helens ahead of them— beacons to mark their way to Portland. After several days, they came to the great valley of the lower Columbia River. Here they had to cross the river again.

"The point at which we struck the Columbia," Grizzly recalled, "was near the Cascades, a few miles below a ferry, to which, after a brief stoppage, we proceeded." The ferryman was a surly Pennsylvanian by the name of Hall. He had a good stout boat made of hewn timbers, but demanded such a large toll—over one hundred dollars—for taking Grizzly's caravan across, that the mountain man indignantly refused. He offered what he considered a reasonable payment of dried meat and furs—even several of the animals; but the ferryman would not agree. Then Grizzly suggested one of his horses as payment, but this offer was scornfully refused as well. Grizzly began to get hot under the collar. If Hall wasn't disposed to do what was fair, he declared, he would take his boat anyway.

The ferryman, his face flushed with anger, swore that he

would do no such thing; Grizzly maintained that he would. The argument grew louder, and Hall started toward his cabin. Grizzly suspected that he was going to get his gun.

Taking his own rifle from his shoulder, he ordered the other to stop. Seeing that Grizzly was serious, the ferryman obeyed. Another session of hard bargaining began, and finally Hall said that he would ferry them across for the best horse in the train. Grizzly would not agree to this, and offered another one.

"There stands a horse worth seventy-five dollars in any market," he said. "If you like to take him, good and well; if not, it cannot be helped."

"I suppose," Hall replied, "if I do not take him, I will get nothing?"

"I know that you will get nothing!" Grizzly responded.

Seeing that Grizzly was dead serious, Hall prepared the boat and took them across in two trips, grumbling all the while. The last Grizzly saw of him, he was leading the traded horse off to his stable.

From that point on, they traveled through country that was just being settled. The strange caravan attracted a great deal of attention wherever it appeared. Upon reaching the outskirts of Portland, they camped in a grove of trees which they made their headquarters while they were in town. The trip had taken nearly a month.

Grizzly needed several days in which to make all the necessary arrangements for his animals and other products. He negotiated with the captain of the bark *Mary Ann* to carry all of his wild animals except Lady Washington to Boston, then supervised their loading and saw to it that sufficient food was taken aboard to feed them during the long voyage. A member of the crew was hired to take care of the animals during the ocean trip, and to see to it that both they and the furs, hides, and other valuables were safely delivered to their proper destinations when the ship reached Boston.

Finally, Adams settled accounts with Kimball, Partridge, and Sykesey, who had elected to stay in Oregon, as well as with the Nez Percé Indians, who were heading back to their village with the tribe's horses, and bid them all farewell. Accompanied only by Stanislaus and Tuolumne, Lady Washington, and the little Indian dog, he headed back toward his old camp in the Sierra Nevada, traveling south from Portland by way of the Willamette Trail.

11

Winter in the Sierra Nevada

It was early October before Grizzly and the two Indians arrived back at his old camp on the headwaters of the Tuolumne and Stanislaus Rivers. Much to his disgust, he found the cabin practically in ruins. The doors which he had fashioned with so much care had been ripped off their hinges and broken. Many of the roof poles had been pulled off and used for firewood. Wild beasts would not have caused such destruction; neither would the local Indians, who were his friends. His fellow white men were the culprits. Everywhere he looked he saw the destructive marks of the ax. There were some men, he reflected bitterly, who would steal everything they could, then smash what they had to leave behind.

Luckily, Grizzly had stored his tools in a nearby cave, and the vandals hadn't found them. He and the two youths set to work, and after several days they had the cabin snug and tight once again. That finished, they built a shelter for the horses, and cut and stacked enough grass to see the animals through the cold months ahead.

Once all these chores were finished to his satisfaction, Grizzly took the mules down to Howard's Ranch. A winter of rest and good pasturage in the lowlands would fatten them up. On the way, he passed through an Indian village whose inhabitants, he soon realized, were of the tribe to which Stanislaus and Tuolumne belonged. The chief inquired about them, and Grizzly related how helpful the boys had been that summer. They were good lads, he assured the Indian leader, and promised that they would soon come down for a visit.

When he returned to camp, Grizzly gave each of the boys a new buckskin suit. He also gave them one of the horses, which they could keep, sell, or trade, as they wished. When he suggested that they take a vacation and visit their people, the swarthy faces of the two Indians lit up with pleasure. They were eager to see their families again. With their wages and new finery, they would have the status of minor chiefs. Strutting like peacocks in their clean new buckskins, they set off with the horse. For the first time in months Grizzly was alone.

For a few days he felt rather lonely. Soon, however, he began to enjoy his solitude. After all, he had the companionship of Lady Washington and Blackie, the little Indian dog that Chief Kennasket had given him. Blackie was a funny-looking little fellow, woolly, short legged, and black as tar. He hadn't grown much, and evidently would always be small.

Lady Washington, however, was the animal that pleased him most. Nearly two years old, she weighed about two hundred and fifty pounds. Her winter coat had grown in, thick and heavy and a very pretty honey color. She was steadfast and affectionate—a far cry from the vicious and defiant creature she had been when he had captured her just four months before. She was with Grizzly all the time; he talked to her in lieu of human company. He would soon get another grizzly—Ben Franklin—that would be his all-time favorite. But the Lady filled the bill that winter of 1853–1854.

"Lady Washington was now a constant companion of all my little excursions," he recalled. "She accompanied me to the scene of my labors, stayed by me while I worked, and followed me when I hunted. The kind and gentle disposition she had begun to exhibit in Washington Territory improved with time and care, and she was now as faithful and devoted, I was going to say, as is possible for any animal to be; but in making this assertion, my noble California grizzly, Ben Franklin, that most excellent of all beasts, must be excepted. But for Ben . . . the Lady could truly be pronounced second to none of all the creatures over which the Creator appointed man to be the lord and master."

One day in early winter, Grizzly was out hunting, the Lady by his side, when he shot a buck mule deer some five miles from camp. It was too heavy a load for him to carry back by himself, so he decided to enlist Lady Washington's help. After gutting and cleaning the deer, he cut it in half and bound one portion on the Lady's broad back. After all, most of the venison would go to feed her, so why shouldn't she carry her own food back to camp. Lady gazed at him with a puzzled look as he bound the side of deer to her. She had carried small packs before, but never a sizeable load like this.

When the load was fastened to Grizzly's satisfaction, he slung the other half of the deer carcass on his shoulder and headed for camp. Instead of following him, as was her usual custom, Lady Washington sat back on her haunches with what seemed like a stubborn expression on her face. She turned and tried to reach back, first with one paw and then with the other, to pull off the side of venison.

Grizzly roared a protest, and at that Lady Washington started forward. But she soon stopped again. Twisting her head around she seized the load with her teeth. Grizzly promptly gave her a smart whack on the snout with a stick, an action he hadn't taken in a long time. Lady Washington growled in surprise, but released the venison. She remembered. For several minutes she padded quietly along beside him. They hadn't gone far, however, before she stopped a third time. Snorting sassily, she lay down in the path and started to roll. "I'll show you!" she as much as said.

In answer, Grizzly cuffed her and gave her a good scolding. Again she got up and followed him. But before long it was the same thing again, and she was rolling over and over like a child having a tantrum. This time, Grizzly gave her several sharp raps with the stick. She was testing him, he realized, trying to see what she could get away with. Well, he wouldn't let her get away with anything! Once she realized that, she would settle down.

And settle down she did—after some more persuasion. By the time they arrived in camp, the Lady was carrying her load with hardly a grumble.

Lady Washington's education continued daily, as Grizzly repaired his old bear traps and built several new ones. Lady Washington soon became accustomed to carrying his blankets and other supplies regularly, as he made his rounds to check and bait the traps.

One day they found a big male grizzly in one of the traps. The bear was in such a bad temper that Grizzly feared it might tear the trap apart if he didn't remain close by to prevent it from doing so. Making a bonfire close to the cage, he and Lady Washington stood guard over the enraged bear. Every once in a while Grizzly had to give his wild captive a poke in the ribs to distract it from tearing up the bottom of the trap.

As quickly as he could, Grizzly built a strong cage of stout timbers for the bear. The next morning, he lashed the cage to the end of the trap and transferred the prisoner with little trouble. Lady Washington stayed by Grizzly all this time, and seemed to look upon her wild relative in much the same way he did. In short, Grizzly considered with a glow of satisfaction, she had truly taken to life as a domestic pet and companion.

A few days later, a female grizzly and her two yearling cubs were caught. Again the forest rang with their outraged roars as Grizzly transferred them to cages. As before, the Lady looked on with only mild interest.

Stanislaus and Tuolumne returned about this time and, with them to look after the traps and the camp, Grizzly took off for Sonora to purchase some needed supplies and to arrange for the sale and transportation of his four recently captured bears. That accomplished, he headed back to his camp on the high slopes. Winter was now fast approaching, and there were many days of cold rain and sleet.

Gradually the rain turned to snow. Grizzly and the two youths were glad to have the snug cabin to sleep in. Above them, the high, jagged peaks of the Sierra Nevada became capped with white. Day by day the snowline crept down the western slopes until it engulfed the camp and went lower. Most of the game retreated to the lowlands ahead of the snow, and Grizzly and his Indian helpers found that they had to travel farther every day in order to find game to feed themselves and their animals.

The going was hard at first when the snow was soft and

new; but, as the temperature plunged lower and lower, a hard crust formed over the drifts, and they found that they could travel over it easily wearing snowshoes. These they made by bending springy, green wood into bows and tying them with rawhide thongs, then weaving strips of fresh, untanned hide over them. Fastened to their moccasins with buckskin loops, the homemade snowshoes were very light and serviceable.

Lady Washington had proved so useful at carrying packs on her back, that Grizzly decided that she could easily haul even heavier loads if he made a sled for her to pull. He and his helpers set to work, and after several days they had a big sled all ready, complete with buckskin harness.

When Grizzly first hitched the Lady to this rig, she looked at him reproachfully, as if asking, what next? She soon got used to it, however, and was a ready helper in hauling loads wherever they went.

One day, Grizzly and Stanislaus were out on a hunt with Lady Washington when a blizzard descended upon them. The wind howled and shrieked through the trees in icy gusts, and the snow swirled down so thick and fast around them that they could scarcely see a dozen feet ahead. Grizzly promptly guided his tiny party to shelter under the low-hanging branches of a big, old pine tree and built a roaring fire. Darkness fell. Huddled in their blankets, they settled down to an uneasy night with heavy snow falling around them. Only Lady Washington seemed comfortable, for she went right to sleep.

Grizzly dozed, but woke after several hours to hear Stanislaus groaning and muttering to himself. The poor fellow was shivering, he discovered, and almost blue with cold. Moving the youth closer to the fire, he promptly added his own blanket to the one already around Stanislaus, and covered him well. Then, adding another pile of wood to the fire, he lay down as close to the flames as he could, and bade the Lady snuggle down close to his back.

At first he was a bit leery that she might turn over in her sleep and crush him, but he soon found that she was quiet. She was a strange bedfellow, he reflected as he dozed off, but a warm one. Her fur was thick, and her big, fat body radiated heat like an oven. Once during the night she got up and withdrew for a few minutes, but soon returned. Sighing sleepily, she licked Grizzly's hand before nestling down beside him once more and going back to sleep. After that night, Grizzly depended on his big pet bear to keep him warm and snug on many a cold winter night.

In this way, Grizzly passed his second winter in the Sierra camp. By the time the snow was in retreat, he had collected a good cache of skins and furs.

12

To Yosemite,
the Valley
of Ahwahnee

At winter's end, the deep white drifts began to melt, and the green of sprouting grass started to show around the cabin. Day by day the snowline retreated toward the mountain summits; earlier every morning the rising sun glowed like fire above the lofty peaks to the east. The sweet and earthy smells of springtime began to perfume the air.

Stanislaus and Tuolumne were delighted at the signs of returning warmth. So, from all appearances, was Lady Washington. Even Grizzly, much as he had enjoyed the solitude of the past winter, worked with a new zest as he got ready for the busy season ahead. This summer he wanted to undertake a long hunting journey to the Rocky Mountains.

One day as he was working around camp, Grizzly heard a faint halloo from far down the slopes. At length a figure appeared. As the man drew closer, Grizzly recognized him as Mr. Solon, an old acquaintance from Sonora.

Around the campfire that evening, Solon told Grizzly that he was going on a month's hunting trip to the Yosemite area, and wondered whether Grizzly would come with him.[15] Solon appreciated the skills of his Massachusetts friend as a hunter and trapper, and knew that his presence would assure a successful trip. Grizzly liked the idea. He hadn't as yet explored the fabled Yosemite region, even though it wasn't far away. The trip would be a welcome diversion before the long summer trip to come.

After a few days of preparation, including a trip to Howard's Ranch to get the mules, they started off, heading southeast across the slopes toward Yosemite. Stanislaus stayed behind to look after the camp, but Tuolumne accompanied Grizzly and Solon. So did Lady Washington, and Queenie, a female greyhound dog that Grizzly had picked up on his visit to Howard's Ranch. Queenie would soon have pups, and Grizzly hoped to rear and train them as hunting dogs.

After three days they reached the beautiful valley that formed the western gateway to Yosemite. Still untouched wilderness, its spectacular scenery was already well known from the descriptions of adventurous forty-niners who had visited it in search of gold. Grizzly was more familiar with the mountain scenery of the Sierra Nevada than the majority of goldseekers, but he had never seen anything to equal Yosemite. He gazed with awe at the sheer cliffs rising a half-mile or more above the green valley, and at the series of breathtaking water falls that foamed over the crests of the rocks and plunged down thousands of feet to the Merced River. The white cascades seemed to fall from the clouds.

After working their way through the valley to a spot about ten miles above the great falls, the hunting party set up a temporary camp and began to explore the area further. Yosemite seemed to be a hunter's paradise. Deer, panthers, bears, and wolves were plentiful, and Grizzly kept eyeing the

Yosemite Fall.

high cliffs for glimpses of bighorn sheep. But no matter how good the hunting was where they were, he wanted to see more of this fabulous region. After a few days he persuaded Solon to move on. Breaking camp, they moved south a few miles and established new headquarters along one of the creeks that formed the headwaters of the Merced. It was here that the newly acquired greyhound bore her pups. And it was here, too, that Grizzly got what would become his most beloved and best-known bear—Ben Franklin.

While hunting by himself one day, he discovered a grizzly bear den on the side of a steep ravine. The opening, about three feet wide, was almost hidden by a clump of bushes, but Grizzly noticed it because of the big pile of excavated dirt, "as much as fifty carloads" such as a miner dumps at the opening of a tunnel.

Grizzly was excited by his discovery. The den looked like the winter shelter of a big, old female, he told himself, a den in which there would likely be cubs. Most male grizzlies would not bother to dig such a big, snug den. He had long dreamed of getting newborn grizzly cubs to raise and tame, shaping their characters just as he wanted. He had Lady Washington, of course, and she was certainly a useful companion. But she had been a yearling when he captured her. What couldn't he do with newborn cubs if he could get them!

Hurrying back to camp, he packed blankets and supplies sufficient for several days on his mule Betz, and carefully cleaned his revolver. He told Solon to hunt without him until he had finished his business with this grizzly bear. Leaving Lady Washington and Queenie with his human companions, he headed back toward the den.

Arriving at the mouth of the ravine, he climbed a tall tree to study the lay of the land. From this lofty lookout, he picked out a good sentinel post for himself, a small clump of junipers about one hundred yards from the den and on the opposite slope of the ravine. Descending, he crawled into the junipers and checked his line of sight. As he had anticipated, it gave him a good view of the mouth of the grizzly den, while the thick foliage concealed him from view. That settled, he tethered the mule some distance away. He fed her and started a little fire for her protection during the night. Then he crept cautiously back into the clump of junipers. Settling himself in his blankets, his rifle at the ready between his knees, he began a long vigil.

Nothing moved within the den opening. Late afternoon shadows crept across the ravine and the sun sank behind the hills. Hour after hour of darkness passed, and Grizzly grimaced with discomfort. The ground around his hiding place was too steep to lie on in any comfort, and the night air was quite chilly. Shivering, he hugged his blankets to him and stared toward the bear den. Nothing stirred in the pale moonlight, nothing made a sound. It was as though all the beasts of the area were avoiding this ravine, the domain of the old she-grizzly.

At length faint streaks of light began to appear in the east. Dawn was on its way at last. Stretching his cramped muscles, Grizzly decided to fire a shot, not only to see what effect the noise might have, but also to put a fresh charge into his rifle. He pulled the trigger, and the report echoed and re-echoed from side to side of the canyon. Almost immediately he heard loud snuffling noises and several muffled whoofs from the den. Climbing a small tree to better observe the entrance, he watched closely for a few moments. The sounds quickly stopped, and no bear came to the den entrance.

Disgruntled, Grizzly once more took up his old post in the junipers. It was almost noon before sunshine entered the narrow ravine and Grizzly crawled out of his hiding place to check on the mule. After watering Betz and moving her to a new pasture, he ate a meal of dried venison. Refreshed, he returned to his vigil with renewed determination. He would outlast that old bear yet, he vowed to himself.

The afternoon wore on. Vultures soared overhead, and a few birds chirped in the chaparral. Perhaps a magpie called in the brush, and a squirrel chattered in a nearby pine. But Grizzly did not see or hear anything within the den. Before dusk, he allowed himself to doze off for several hours. He needed to be wide awake tonight. The old bear would surely come out.

The shivering vigil of the second night was almost like that of the first. Near daybreak Grizzly once again heard snuffling sounds from within the den. Firing his rifle, as he had done the day before, he was rewarded by a low, rumbling growl. In a moment the shaggy head of a big grizzly bear filled the entrance. Grizzly waited for her to come out. But after blinking and peering to either side for several minutes, she retreated back into the depths. At the same time, Grizzly unmistakably heard the yelping of cubs. There *were* young ones with her! He vowed he'd get them if it took all spring.

After two fruitless all-night vigils, Grizzly decided that it was time to change his tactics. He would move up on the old bear and force the issue. Before putting his new plan into action, though, he crept out to feed and water the mule, and ate his own meal of pemmican. Then he went back to his sentinel post in the junipers. Starting from this post, he began to crawl toward the den. He took extra pains to move quietly, without snapping even a twig. If the she-bear came out while he was crawling through the brush on his hands and knees, she'd have him for sure.

Worming his way across the rough ground, he reached a clump of bushes scarcely forty yards from the den. So far, so good. He had an almost perfect view of the entrance from this new spot, except for several small branches in his way. Reluctantly laying his rifle aside for the first time in two days, he inched forward and carefully cut them away. He'd be a goner if the bear came out now. The skin at the nape of his neck prickled at the thought. Inching his way back, he sighed with relief at the feel of the Kentucky rifle in his hand once more.

As evening approached, Grizzly made a quick trip back to the mule, but did not linger to light a fire for her. He headed quickly back to his new outpost. Wrapping himself in his blankets, he began his third night of watching and waiting. He was certain that the issue would be resolved tonight. He'd felt the same way, he remembered, just before he captured Lady Washington.

Hour after hour of shivering darkness passed and, in spite of his determination not to, Grizzly fell asleep. The two previous nights without any real rest had taken their toll. It was nearly dawn when he was suddenly wakened by a loud, screeching wail. Startled, he grabbed for his rifle and peered wildly at the den entrance. No bear. Then he looked quickly about in every direction. Nothing was stirring. Gradually his thumping heart calmed down, as he realized what it was he had heard. Just a panther yowling! What a fool you are to be startled by a cowardly, sneaking cat, he thought to himself.

Daylight came, but there was no sign of life around the bear den. Grizzly was still angry at himself for having fallen asleep. That old bear might have left her den while he was dreaming. Thoroughly disgusted with himself, he determined to bring matters to a head without further delay. If she was in that den, he'd get her out, one way or another.

Sticking a few leafy branches into the folds of his cap for camouflage, he settled himself as inconspicuously as possible in his hiding place. Then he took a deep breath and let go with a wild yell that sounded through the ravine like a war whoop. Immediately there was an answering whoof from the den, and in a moment the huge old she-bear padded out through the entrance and peered about suspiciously. Growling, she stood up on her hind feet to get a better look. To Grizzly, she looked at least ten feet tall. He hardly breathed for fear she would notice him and charge. The old bear soon dropped to all fours and sat down, facing away from him. No position for a decisive shot.

Grizzly gave a short, sharp whistle. The big bear whirled about and once again rose on her hind legs, facing him. This was the moment! Taking careful aim, Grizzly fired. The bear staggered backward a couple of steps and dropped to the ground, blood flowing from her breast. She snorted and began to bite and claw at the earth—a sure sign that she was in a bad way.

Dropping his rifle, Grizzly leaped over the bushes toward her, his Colt revolver in one hand and his bowie knife in the other. As he rushed forward, the old bear stood up once more. Teeth bared and snarling, she charged toward him from a distance of just thirty feet. Grizzly emptied his revolver into her, pumping out the six shots in rapid succession. With a tremendous sigh his shaggy opponent sank to the ground, blood spurting from her many wounds, her long claws raking the dirt. Leaping forward, Grizzly thrust his knife into her side again and again. The enormous, furry body shuddered, then lay still. The mother bear was dead at last.

Grizzly felt shaken as he looked down at his valiant opponent. He gazed at the silent hills and at the sky, where a lone vulture soared, a speck in the heavens. Mixed feelings churned within him: regret at having killed a beast that had tried so courageously to protect her young; joy that what he had dreamed of was now within his grasp. He would have newborn grizzly cubs to tame and train.

13

Ben
Franklin

Grizzly slowly approached the entrance of the den and peered into it. He couldn't see or hear anything. He paused for a moment as a thought crossed his mind: maybe there was another adult bear in the den. But just as quickly he brushed the idea aside. It didn't make sense. No she-bear with cubs would tolerate another adult bear anywhere near them. On the other hand, he had better be ready, just in case.

He carefully reloaded his rifle and revolver. Then he lit a torch of dried pine splints. Laying his rifle at the ready in the mouth of the den, he got down on his hands and knees and crawled in, the pistol in his right hand, the torch in his left. The entranceway went straight back for six or eight feet, then opened into a spacious room some eight feet in diameter and five feet high.

Holding the torch in front of him, Grizzly peered eagerly about the den. The floor was covered with a thick bed of dried leaves and grass, but he couldn't see anything else except the flickering shadows cast on the wall by his torch. For a moment he had a sickening feeling of disappointment. Were there no cubs after all? Then he heard a slight rustling and saw something move in a corner of the den. His heart surged when he made out two tiny cubs. Scooping them up, he thrust them into his buckskin shirt, next to his inner, woolen shirt, and quickly crawled outside.

In the bright light of day, he took out the cubs to examine them. Hardly bigger than squirrels, the two baby grizzly bears had silky coats of very fine hair. Their eyes were closed, and their tiny ears lay close to their heads. No more than a week old, Grizzly figured. Both were males. He watched with satisfaction as they twisted and rolled on the ground, squeaking softly as they nuzzled here and there in search of their mother. They were lively youngsters—healthy and perfect.

Picking them up, he gently put them back into his buckskin shirt and headed toward the place where he had tethered the mule. Once he had skinned the big grizzly and loaded one of her hams on old Betz, it would be time to head back to camp.

When he reached the spot where he had left Betz the afternoon before, he was surprised to find her gone. Only her broken tether was still there. Looking about, Grizzly saw several dark stains on the ground. Blood. He frowned, remembering the panther of the night before. Had it gotten her?

The mule's tracks were easy to follow, and Grizzly trailed them up the slope and over the peak of the neighboring hill. At the bottom of the next ravine he spotted the mule, grazing.

"Betz!" he called. The mule pricked up her ears and snorted. For a moment Grizzly thought she would take off.

He spoke to her again as he hurried toward her, and she seemed to recognize his voice. Nickering, she turned and waited. She was trembling, Grizzly noted, and there were several deep scratches on her flanks.

Mounting her, Adams returned to the grizzly den, where he skinned and gutted the old bear. Cutting up her flesh, he loaded part of it on the mule. Leaving the remainder to be picked up later, he headed back for camp. Darkness had fallen by the time he arrived.

When Grizzly showed Solon and Tuolumne the two squirming cubs, their excited reaction was everything he could have wished for. Choosing one of the cubs for himself, he gave the other to Solon. His friend thought that this was more than generous, but Grizzly reminded him that they had agreed to split whatever they got, share and share alike. Solon finally assented. Then, with many embellishments, Grizzly told the other two how he had stood vigil at the bear den for three days before finally killing the old bear and getting the cubs. By the time he had finished his story, the campfire was nothing but dying embers. Time to sleep. Before turning in for the night, Solon remarked that he would name his cub General Jackson.

"General Jackson was a great man in his way," Grizzly replied, "but I'll call my bear Ben Franklin—a greater name."

The next morning, Grizzly prepared a mixture of flour, water, and sugar—the best he could come up with as a milk substitute for the cubs. He had raised fawns and black bear cubs on this formula in the past. It should work with grizzly cubs, too, at least for a short period of time. Gently forcing open Ben Franklin's tiny jaws, he let a few drops of the mixture trickle into his mouth. The cub spluttered and sneezed, turning his head away, but Grizzly persisted. Solon watched for a few moments and then began to feed General Jackson in the same way. It was some time, however, before they got much nourishment into the little, round bellies.

Grizzly tucked the cubs back into the box nest he had fixed up for them, and gave Tuolumne instructions about their care during the day. Then, he and Solon ate their own breakfast and set out to pick up the rest of the bear meat.

When they arrived at the den, Grizzly was surprised to see that most of the meat was gone. He had left it near the entrance, and wolves or vultures must have taken it. Since Solon was curious to see where the cubs had been born, Grizzly then lit a pine torch and started to lead the way into the den. He stopped when he heard a low growl ahead of him. By the light of the torch he could just make out the figure of a big wolf sitting on its haunches at the back of the den.

After warning his companion of the situation, he declared that he was going to go after the wolf. Solon was to stand ready, he instructed, in case the wolf got past him. Without further ado, he crawled back into the den and fired at the wolf with his revolver. He missed in the dim light and, with a sudden bound, the wolf swept past him and dashed toward the entranceway. Grizzly grabbed at the wolf's tail as it passed him, and slashed at its side with his knife. He missed again. But Solon was ready and waiting outside. As the wolf burst through the den opening, he clubbed it over the head with a stout limb he had snatched up. The wolf fell without a sound.

After congratulating Solon on his timely action, Grizzly gave the torch to his friend and told him to go into the den and have a look around for himself. When Solon was halfway into the den, Adams, always the practical joker, let out a sudden whoop, shouting to him to watch out for the other wolf.

Crawling into the den from which he had obtained his bear cub,
Ben Franklin, Adams is confronted by a wolf.

Startled, Solon scuttled out backward as fast as he could,
and Grizzly roared with laughter. Unsurprisingly, Solon
failed to see any humor in the prank. In fact, he was quite
angry. Grizzly quickly made amends as best he could, and
Solon calmed down. Then both of them entered the den and

examined the birthplace of Ben Franklin and General Jackson.

When they got back to camp, Grizzly noted that the cubs were tumbling restlessly in their nest, making soft, whimpering sounds. They were hungry, that was certain. The men tried giving them the flour, water, and sugar mixture, as before, but the cubs squirmed and twisted and tried to push the food away. Grizzly realized that this method of feeding the cubs wasn't working. He gazed at the two little bears with some frustration. What to do?

He glanced at Queenie, the greyhound, who was nursing her week-old puppies nearby. Grizzly had already considered enlisting her as the cubs' foster mother, but had discarded the idea for fear the dog might turn on the tiny bear cubs and harm them. Now he decided to chance it. The men would keep a close watch on the dog, and see what happened. There was, however, one other concern. Queenie had plenty of milk for her own pups, but in all probability did not have enough for the cubs as well. He hated to do it, but "to make room, we destroyed all the greyhound pups except one," he later admitted.

Carrying a cub in each hand, Grizzly approached the dog and laid the little bears down beside her, near the remaining puppy. For a moment Queenie looked at them with wide and wary eyes. Then, hair bristling, she curled her lips and bared her teeth in an angry snarl. Suddenly she lunged at the cubs, snapping and biting. Watching for such action, Grizzly quickly restrained the dog and soothed her. It took some doing, but Queenie gradually became used to the cubs.

". . . by degrees she admitted them freely," Adams observed with satisfaction, "and would even lap and fondle them, so that . . . they at last shared in her affection with her own offspring."

Although they were very young, the two cubs already had sharp claws. To prevent them from scratching Queenie or the puppy, which Grizzly had named Rambler, he made little buckskin mittens for the cubs to wear while they nursed. They were about the same size as the week-old pup when Grizzly first got them, but the little bears grew much faster than he did. They were thriving on the milk of their foster mother. After a few days, Grizzly began to bruise meat to make it tender, and feed bits of it to the cubs. Once they started to eat meat, it wasn't long before they were weaned.

14

Attacked
by a Panther

During the next two weeks Solon made several trips to the nearest mines to sell game to the prospectors. The others continued to hunt while he was away. In his spare time, Grizzly made a saddle out of green hide for Lady Washington, so that she could carry supplies more efficiently on their daily jaunts. With the saddle strapped to her back, she could easily pack two hundred pounds of meat or equipment.

Grizzly enjoyed these days to the fullest. There was nothing to do except hunt and explore this beautiful wilderness! On one hunting trip he captured two mule deer fawns; on another, a couple of month-old wolf pups. He was sure all would fetch good prices.

One day, when Solon had returned from his most recent trip to the mines, he and Grizzly went out together on a hunt. Exploring a broad valley, they came to a place where it forked into two ravines, separated by a wooded ridge. Grizzly explored one ravine while Solon explored the other. Adams had been by himself for a half hour or more when he

110

heard a faint shout from the other ravine. Solon. The distance could not hide the note of desperation in his friend's voice as he cried for help. Grizzly hurried up the side of the ridge as fast as he could go, and over the crest. Solon was in some sort of serious trouble.

He heard another cry. Peering about, he finally spotted Solon lying on the ground some distance away. A big panther was on top of him, biting at his back and shoulder. Calling to his friend to lie still, Grizzly took careful aim at the panther with his rifle. He was fearful of hitting Solon, however, and aimed high when he fired. At the report of the rifle, the big, tawny cat jumped from Solon's back. Tail lashing back and forth, it looked about and snarled, then bounded away.[16]

Without stopping to reload, Grizzly hurried down the slope. Solon was covered with blood and moaning. He seemed to be in bad shape. Quickly stripping off his companion's shirt, Grizzly saw that his back and shoulder were marked with many deep slashes inflicted by the panther's claws and teeth. His neck was badly bitten, but he had been lucky—no vital blood vessels were torn. His friend was not mortally wounded.

Solon had been walking along looking for game, he explained to Grizzly, when he was suddenly hurled to the ground by the big cat leaping onto his back. It must have been lying in wait on an overhead branch, he figured. He'd had the presence of mind to pull his heavy buckskin shirt over his neck. That had probably saved him.

Leading Solon to a nearby stream, Grizzly made him bend over the bank while he administered his favorite remedy for serious wounds—icy-cold water.[17] He poured water over Solon's neck and back until the other man cried for mercy, swearing that he was freezing to death. But Grizzly was firm. He continued the treatment for another few minutes, then eased Solon back into his wool shirt and buckskins. He added his own buckskin shirt on top of those, and soaked the lot of them with cold water. He also insisted that Solon drink as much water as possible. His friend would soon become warm, he explained, and the water would make him perspire more readily; that would help to ease the pain.

Solon complained bitterly about the cold water treatment, but on the way back to camp he admitted that he already felt better than he had thought he would. Once in camp, Grizzly checked him over once more, and announced that he wasn't satisfied with his work. There were several deep scalp wounds on the side of Solon's head that needed further attention. But first Grizzly had to cut Solon's hair.

His bowie knife was the closest thing to a pair of shears any of them had, so Grizzly resolutely set to work with it. Although Solon howled in protest and yelped in pain that Grizzly's cure was worse than the panther's bite, Tuolumne held the indignant patient's head while Grizzly resolutely hacked away at his hair until it was "short as the nap of velvet" around the wounds. Finally, Grizzly applied the cold water treatment and the compresses once more.

The next morning, Solon admitted that Grizzly's treatment may have helped him. Aside from some stiffness and soreness, he felt as well as could be expected. He decided to stay in camp and take it easy, however, while Grizzly and Tuolumne set off to try to track down the panther and kill it.

The two of them soon reached the spot where Solon had been attacked. Following the panther's trail was easy enough, for there was a spot of blood every few feet. My shot yesterday didn't miss after all, Grizzly reflected.

They tracked the big cat more than a mile, and finally

entered a narrow canyon with steep rock walls and a thick growth of scrubby trees in its bottom. As they crept slowly through the underbrush, they heard a low growl ahead of them. Stopping, they peered through the vegetation and finally spotted the panther lying in a shallow rock cave near the base of the ravine. Grizzly could make out several cubs beside her.

Beckoning Tuolumne to come up beside him, Grizzly whispered to him to fire first. It would give his helper confidence, he thought. He'd hold his own fire, but be ready to back him up if necessary. Taking careful aim, Tuolumne fired. The shot struck the old panther, but did not kill her. The big cat turned to flee, but Grizzly fired, and she fell to the ground dead. Plunging quickly ahead, Grizzly and Tuolumne scooped up five little spotted kittens—only a few days old. After skinning the old panther, they headed back to camp.

When they got there, Solon complained of being lonesome. It was easy to see that he had been brooding over his wounds and his inactivity. Grizzly held up the panther skin, and Solon's face lighted up. After showing him the panther cubs, Grizzly related how they had tracked and killed his attacker of the day before.

Feeding the panther kittens would be a problem, Grizzly allowed, but he was determined to keep them. There were too many of them for Queenie to nurse. He'd already made her the foster mother to the two grizzly cubs; enough was enough. Tuolumne was doing a good job helping to take care of the fawns and wolf pups. With his assistance, they'd manage the kittens as well.

The care of so many young animals was quite time-consuming, and Grizzly soon decided that they should head for home. The animals they had captured—two wolf pups, two

fawns, the two grizzly bear cubs, and the five panther kits—
were put into boxes or baskets and carried on either side of
the horses and mules.

Lady Washington carried her share of the cargo, too. She
grumbled a bit when several lively panther kittens were
slung over her back in baskets, but didn't protest further
until they began to whimper and cry. Then she became very
uneasy, and Grizzly was worried that she might lie down
and roll over. He stroked her and talked to her soothingly,
and she soon calmed down. When her master led her by her
collar, she followed quietly.

It took only several days travel, in easy stages, before they
were back at their old Sierra camp.

15

Expedition to the Rocky Mountains

Grizzly immediately began to prepare for the long trip to the Rocky Mountains. Provisions and supplies had to be purchased; equipment needed to be checked and repaired, and a number of the animals captured in Yosemite had to be sold or taken to Howard's Ranch for the summer.

Despite Grizzly's urging that Solon come along with him to the Rockies, his friend decided to return to Sonora. In his stead, Grizzly recruited an old mining acquaintance from Chinese Camp for his second-in-command, a young Mississippian named Gray. The southerner had often told Adams that he would like to accompany him on a long hunting expedition. Now he jumped at the chance. Grizzly, for his part, felt fortunate to have him along. Gray was a good shot and an experienced hunter. He had a naturally cheerful and optimistic nature, and was hardy and vigorous. With a curly, black beard, sweeping handlebar moustache, and long, black hair, he made a striking figure. He assured Grizzly that he was ready for whatever they might encounter.

Grizzly said that Gray should have one-third of the profits of whatever they might get in the Rockies. Gray already carried a thousand-dollars worth of gold dust with him in a leather pouch tucked inside his shirt. Eventually he wanted to return to his native Mississippi, he told Grizzly, and might very well head for home at the end of the summer, after the hunt was over.

It was almost April by now, and the snow had already receded from the lower slopes of the mountains. Time to be on their way. A band of about twenty-five Digger Indians were camped not far from Grizzly's cabin; when they learned that he planned to cross the Sierra Nevada, they begged to accompany him as far as the lakes on the other side. They wanted to fish there during the spring. Grizzly reluctantly agreed. He was on good terms with the local tribes, but these Diggers looked like a primitive and ragtail bunch, and he didn't want to be held back by them. But Providence had created them for some purpose, he reasoned, and ". . . it was the part of philosophy and wisdom to take them as they were and make the best of them."

On the day they were to leave, Grizzly got up at dawn and roused his companions. All the necessary supplies and equipment were packed in the wagon, which also held Ben Franklin and the pup, Rambler. Lady Washington was chained to the rear of the wagon, while Queenie and Blackie, the Indian dog, ran free. The wagon's pulling power consisted of the two mules in the lead, followed by the two yoked oxen.

The rays of the rising sun were just beginning to show over the crests of the mountains when Grizzly and his party started on their long journey, following the middle fork of the Tuolumne River. The ragged procession of Indians followed a short distance behind. That night they camped near the river's source. Over the next five days the going got increasingly difficult as they climbed higher and higher into the mountains.

There was still plenty of snow at these high altitudes, and in some areas the crusted drifts were five feet deep, or more. Soon, any outward sign of the primitive trail became nonexistent; in many places the slopes were so steep that it seemed impossible for the wagon to go on. Grizzly issued shovels and pickaxes to the Indians, however, and organized them into roadworkers. In some places they cut trails through the steep slopes of snow so the wagon could pass; in others, they dragged the wagon forward by ropes.

The fourth night out was bitterly cold, and nearly everyone was exhausted by the backbreaking work. They camped that night under a huge pine tree. A roaring fire was built, and Grizzly set his crew to roasting huge quantities of venison, "none too much, however, for the ravenous crowd around it." Revived, the Diggers sang and danced after supper, in high good spirits. Finally they bedded down to sleep—men, women, and children all huddled together for warmth.

The same backbreaking toil continued the next day. At one point, the passage through a canyon was so narrow that the wagon had to be taken off its bed, and the Indians carried it and the supplies through, piece by piece. Late on the afternoon of the sixth day they reached the summit of the Sierra Nevada, and camped for the night a short distance down the eastern slope.

At dawn, Grizzly walked back to the highest point of land, and from this lofty spot gazed in all directions. The high ridges of the mountains glittered white in the early morning sun, then flushed pink and crimson as the sun rose higher in the sky. To the west, hazy and faint in the shaded

Summit of the Sierra Nevada.

distance, he could see the wide central valley of California. To the east, he saw gentle hills and sunlit plains, with barren stretches of the Great American Desert beyond them.

Adams felt deep satisfaction as he gazed over the jagged peaks they had struggled through. His mind flashed back over all the difficulties they had overcome in the past few days. "I claim no great credit for leading my army over the California Alps," he recalled, "but perhaps my difficulties were in proportion as great as were those of Hannibal or Napoleon." Those two historic leaders might well have disagreed with this observation, but that would not have bothered John Adams.[18]

The party started down the eastern slopes of the mountains in high spirits. Near evening they came to a deserted log cabin built the summer before by traders from Sonora— men intent on doing business with emigrants from the East. After camping there for the night, they continued their descent the next morning. They passed through the snow belt that day and came once again into warm spring weather. That evening they camped in the eastern foothills.

Grizzly decided that his troops needed several days of recuperation after the hard crossing of the mountains. Some of the Indians had frostbitten feet and blistered hands, and everyone needed a rest. He and Gray, together with Stanislaus and Tuolumne, went antelope hunting, and that evening they had a big feast. After eating their fill, the Indians again began to dance. Entering into the spirit of the celebration, Gray got up and tried to imitate the steps of an Indian brave, a sight that amused all the Diggers. Grizzly felt stirred to demonstrate "how the Yankees used to dance when I was a boy; but my gray head and long white beard ill-comported with the lightness of my heels, and the Indians, particularly the squaws, almost burst with laughter at the figure I made, so that I soon resumed my seat and my old pipe, fully satisfied that my dancing days were over."

The next morning they headed on in good spirits, and for a few days they had comparatively easy going. The Emigrant's Trail led them in a northerly direction to Walker's River in what is now western Nevada.[19] Here the Indians remained, except for two young braves who elected to accompany Grizzly to the Rockies. They would rejoin their tribesmen that fall in California.

Continuing northward, Grizzly and his companions crossed forty miles of dry desert before reaching the Carson River, which they followed eastward for two days. At the great bend of the river, they crossed on a raft which they built of cottonwood logs. Ahead, dim in the distance, lay the mysterious Humboldt Mountains, sixty or eighty miles to the north. Grizzly had heard from emigrants that they were the home of many strange animals, including purple panthers and black and white wolves. After four days of travel across desert country, they reached the mountains. They skirted them for some fifteen miles until they came to a narrow canyon that led into a beautiful valley. Grizzly decided to camp in this place for a week or two to rest both the animals and his companions.

He was very pleased with the way his pets had faced the trip so far. Lady Washington, usually tied to the rear axletree of the wagon, had caused no trouble at all. She often accompanied Grizzly on short side trips to hunt, and would carry the meat on her back when they returned to camp. Ben and Rambler were thriving, too. The bear had now far outstripped his canine brother in size, but they still played together happily. Grizzly had carried them in the wagon to this point, but they were getting so active and lively that he decided to let them roam free part of the time. They romped together, and chased jack rabbits and prairie dogs. Rambler's mother, the patient greyhound, began to teach them to hunt.

Grizzly was determined to get some of the panthers of the Humboldt Mountains. If they were indeed purple, and so a different variety, they would be rare prizes. He had heard the big cats shrieking at night in the hills surrounding camp, but had not seen any of them.

One morning, one of the Indian boys told him that they had discovered a panther's den with young ones in it. Grizzly and the others set out for the den at once, and arrived at what seemed to Adams ". . . a perfect Golgotha of the animal creation," with bones of deer and other animals scattered about it.[20] Concealing themselves nearby, they waited. At sundown, two old panthers came out of the den and began to play. Soon three spotted cubs joined them. At a signal, both Gray and Adams fired at the adults. One of them fell dead, but the other one ran away. The cubs quickly retreated into the den.

After making a large fire at the entrance, Grizzly armed himself with a pine torch and a knife, and crawled into the den to get the kittens. Gray followed close behind him. Finally Grizzly spotted the little panthers huddled in a corner of the cave, their eyes glowing with reflected light as they spit their defiance. Scrambling forward, the two men threw their buckskins over the young cats and, in a moment, wrapped them up in their arms.

When he had examined the kittens outside the den, Grizzly realized, much to his disappointment, that they looked just like all the other young panthers he had ever seen. And the hide of the old panther was not purple at all—just the usual tawny color. He kept the cats, however.

Several days later, they were near the panther den again,

and decided to explore it at length. Entering the cave with pine torches, Adams and Gray passed through a narrow opening into a second cave, and from that into a third. It seemed a regular labyrinth. "A panther!" Gray suddenly shouted. Grizzly heard a low growl immediately ahead of him, then saw two flaming eyes. Pointing his pistol between the two glowing eyes, he fired. The big cat screeched loudly, then bounded past him and out of the cave. He and Gray scrambled out in pursuit of the panther as quickly as they could, for the moment paying no attention to the kittens they had glimpsed in the lair. In spite of their efforts, the big cat escaped.

Grizzly then told Gray to go back into the cave and catch the kittens while he guarded the outside against the return of the other big cat. Uneasy at this proposal, Gray refused. There could be other old panthers in the den.

"This circumstance," Grizzly said, "afforded me an opportunity, not only of ridiculing his fears, but of testing his faithfulness in the hour of need." Taking a torch in one hand and his knife in the other, Grizzly told Gray to stand guard outside the den while he crawled in to get the cubs himself.

Reaching the panther's nest, he found five spotted kittens and carefully placed them inside his coat. Doubling it into a sack, he started out. Then Grizzly's taste for practical jokes took over. Upon reaching the entrance where Gray stood guard, he stuck his head out, twisted his face into an expression of agonizing pain, and cried out to his companion, begging him for help.

"What's the matter?" Gray shouted, rushing forward.

"The panther! The panther!" Grizzly pleaded. "Pull me out." Adams twisted his body from side to side and squirmed about, as if a panther had him by the leg. Gray quickly seized his arms and pulled him out.

Jumping to his feet, Adams slapped Gray on the back and congratulated him, remarking that ". . . though he had acted the coward before, he had fully redeemed himself by his prompt action now." Gray, however, did not think much of either Adams's humor or his testing.

The next morning the weather was so beautiful—sunny and warm, with not a cloud to be seen—that Grizzly turned out all his young animals in the grass together. He'd never had such a fine time, he thought, as he watched Ben Franklin, Rambler, and the panther cubs, growling in mock fights, wrestling and playing with one another.

Clouds swept over the mountains that afternoon, though, "like huge banks of snow." As Grizzly watched, the sky grew darker, minute by minute, and the clouds became black. A storm was on its way. He felt a whisper of wind which quickly increased to a gale. Huge hailstones pelted down and torrents of rain began to fall. A tremendous whirlwind appeared on the horizon and began to sweep toward them. There wasn't time for the men to do more than lie flat on the ground with their blankets over them for protection before the cyclone was upon them. The great twister turned the wagon over, scattered gear and supplies, and tore up several nearby trees, throwing them about like sticks. As quickly as it came, the storm passed. After gazing at the scene of confusion and wreckage for a few moments, Grizzly and the others began to gather up their scattered gear and set things in order.

That evening another storm approached. Working against time, Grizzly and his companions unpacked the wagon, turned it over as a shelter, and put their gear beneath it. They placed the animals in sheltering bushes, and crawled into the thick underbrush themselves. Claps of thunder rolled across the sky and bolts of lightning flashed beneath the black clouds. Torrents of rain fell, as before. But the storm quickly passed, and the men and animals, although wet and uncomfortable, were unharmed.

The next morning dawned bright and clear. The men put everything to rights once again, and spent the next several days hunting and drying meat to replenish their dwindling supplies. They refilled all of their waterbags and vessels as well, for they would need all the water they could carry for the long trip of several hundred miles across the Great Basin to the Great Salt Lake.

The forbidding desert and salt flats ahead of them proved the most difficult lap of the whole trip, except for the snowy crossing of the high Sierra. When they started, Grizzly allowed Ben Franklin to travel afoot, along with the dogs. He and Rambler were constant companions. After two days of travel, they were lucky enough to find a camping place where they could refill their water bags. The next day, however, they went on through dry, volcanic country where the only vegetation they encountered was a few clumps of sage. The sun blazed down mercilessly. They searched in vain that evening for a spring, for they had already used up all the water they had carried with them. After a night of torment, they went on, all of them suffering from thirst and the terrible heat.

Scouting ahead, Grizzly spied several slight hills where he thought water might be found. He went back to inform the others, then sent Gray and the Indians ahead to drink while he remained behind to drive the suffering oxen and mules forward, mainly by his own will power. Finally they reached the hills and found a brackish and evil-smelling spring.

Bad as the water was, it brought life back to both the animals and men. They stayed at the spring for two days to regain their strength before struggling onward through the desert. Neither that day nor the next did they find any more water. The animals were all suffering, especially the oxen. And Adams had to admit that he didn't even know where they were. They had lost their way. Alarmed at the plight of both the animals and men, Grizzly explored ahead that night and early morning, searching for the slightest sign of water. At last he discovered a brackish spring some ten miles ahead. It took all day for the exhausted party to reach it.

To add to his other concerns, Grizzly noted that Ben Franklin's paws were bleeding and raw from sharp rocks and hot desert sands. He was reluctant to put him back in the wagon, however, for the young bear had become so accustomed to running free with Rambler that Grizzly knew he would try to get out. He therefore made moccasins for Ben, using elk hide for the soles and buckskin for the uppers. Bound tightly to the cub's feet, they protected them very well.

After resting at the spring for several days, they continued their journey. They had already traveled two hundred miles or more from the Humboldt Mountains, and it wasn't long before they reached what Grizzly believed had to be the shores of Utah Lake, south of Great Salt Lake. Here the change in the country was almost unbelievable—from barren desert to a green land that offered abundant food. They reveled in the grass they found in this region, and the plentiful supplies of good clean water. Passing around the head of the lake, they made their way north toward the Emigrant Trail, hunting buffalo and other game as they progressed.

Some sixty miles east of Salt Lake City, they finally set up their summer camp. June was nearly gone now, and two and a half months had passed since they had left their old camp on the headquarters of the Stanislaus and Tuolumne Rivers.

16

The Courtship
of Lady Washington

The spot where Grizzly Adams camped was close to the place where the Emigrant or California Trail[21] crossed the Muddy Fork of the Green River—today, the extreme southwest corner of Wyoming. Jim Bridger, a well-known mountain man of that time, had his fort and trading post a few miles to the east. There the westbound Emigrant Trail divided: the southern fork led to Salt Lake City and California, while the other fork took the traveler northward to the Snake River and the Oregon Trail. Since 1849, a constant flow of traffic—covered wagons, horse trains, and families on foot—had headed west over these trails in the spring, summer, and fall.

"It had been my intention in traveling to the Rocky Mountains," Grizzly recalled, "not only to hunt and collect animals, but also to trade with that great stream of migrating humanity, which, in search of the gold-bearing hills or the stock-raising valleys of California, poured over the Rocky Mountains by thousands during the whole summer."

126

Pioneers crossing the plains.

But first he wanted to visit Salt Lake City, the new metropolis started just several years before by the Mormons on
the shores of Great Salt Lake.[22] On July 1, he and his companions headed for the city, taking along hides, furs, and
meat, as well as two panther cubs, two wolf pups, and two
fawns, to sell. They would celebrate the Fourth of July in
Salt Lake City. They disposed of most of their meat before
reaching their destination, indeed gave much of it away to
"wayworn and weary sufferers" who roused Adams's sym-

pathy. Once in the settlement, they sold the rest of their supplies and disposed of the young animals at good prices. Then they set out to explore Salt Lake City.

Grizzly looked with approval at the wide, straight streets and sidewalks, with ditches beside them for drainage. Each block was partitioned into house lots, most of them occupied by neat, one-story, adobe houses. There were a few brick houses in the center of town, as well as the Mormon Temple. Grizzly could not help but be impressed by what these people were doing in their "Promised Land."

"It has been usual to call these singular people fanatics," he observed, ". . . but when it is considered that all the world is more or less fanatical . . . I can hardly look upon the Mormons with what is generally considered orthodox contempt. . . . their wonderful labors in their Rocky Mountain city attest the fact that there is at least earnestness and vigor in their counsels."

He had no such favorable view of the Mormon leader, Brigham Young. "I heard Brigham Young preach one day . . . I went to the castle, or the temple as they called it, to listen to Young. He was a great, fat, pursy individual . . . a sort of human compound of fish, flesh, fowl, and other good things generally. . . . He was heaven all over, he seemed to intimate, and all who wanted to go to heaven had only to go to him. He spoke as if he and his Maker were on very intimate terms, indeed, and had no secrets from each other. . . . I never heard so much blasphemous bombast in my life." When shortly afterward Grizzly caught a small black bear cub—a screeching bear, as settlers in the area called the species—Adams remarked that "he contrived to yell and screech with wonderful energy and tirelessness . . . he put me in mind of Brigham Young's exhortations. . . . I christened him, on the spot, after the Mormon prophet."

* * *

After the holiday celebration in Salt Lake City, Grizzly was happy to get back to the comparative quiet of camp. He could hold his own again in company with civilization, but he still preferred primitive surroundings and wild companions.

He had camped in the middle of good buffalo country, and for a week or more Grizzly and his companions hunted the big, shaggy beasts, collecting the meat and hides, and selling supplies to the emigrants. Lady Washington was pressed into service as a pack animal for the meat, and the eyes of many travelers widened at the sight of the big bear carrying supplies on her back.

Grizzly couldn't resist adding several buffalo calves to his wild menagerie. He either lassoed them, or simply allowed hungry orphan calves to follow him back to camp, where he tethered and fed them.

Always ready for new places, new adventures, he soon got the wanderlust again. Striking camp, he headed northward past Fort Bridger, and set up new headquarters at Ham's Fork, on the bend of the Bear River.

The new location was close to the heavily traveled Oregon Trail, so Grizzly set up a continuous night guard. Two men would be on duty until midnight, another two until dawn. Ben Franklin and the younger animals were confined— either chained, or secured in light cages near the place where Grizzly slept. Lady Washington, as usual, was chained to a tree near the edge of the campgrounds.

When Grizzly wakened one morning, Tuolumne told him of an interesting occurrence that had happened during the night. He and one of the new Indian helpers had been on guard from midnight on, and while they were on duty a strange wild grizzly bear had come to camp. It had been

Western North America, showing the Oregon, California, and Gila River Trails, and many of the places Adams visited on his expeditions during the 1850s.

very interested in Lady Washington, Tuolumne said, and had visited with her for an hour or so, as quiet and friendly as you please, before leaving peaceably. The bear had been so civil that the guards had not thought it necessary to waken their leader. Grizzly was very interested to hear about it, however, and told the two Indians to let him know immediately if the bear should come again.

The next night Grizzly was awakened by a touch on his arm. Instantly alert, he peered up to see Tuolumne bending over him. Rising silently, Grizzly picked up his rifle and followed the youth to his guard post.

A pale moon shown through the trees. By its position, Grizzly realized that it was early morning, not yet an hour past midnight. Settling down beside Tuolumne, he peered through the shadows toward the spot where Lady Washington was chained, her shaggy suitor beside her. Grizzly watched to see what would happen.

The strange bear stayed with Lady Washington until dawn before ambling away. The next night he appeared for a third time, and ". . . like a loyal lover, he was very attentive," Grizzly noted. He had a friendly feeling for this suitor of the Lady's, and wished him well. "Gray advised that he should be killed; but I opposed the proposition, and, for what I know, he still roams in his native haunts." After that night the male grizzly appeared no more. He had been successful in his courtship, and Adams looked forward to the day the Lady would present him with cubs.

Out hunting with Gray and Stanislaus a few days later, Grizzly came upon fresh bear tracks in a ravine. Crawling slowly forward through the thick brush, the three of them finally spotted an old she-bear playing with her cubs in a shallow pool. After watching them for a while, Grizzly fired at the mother bear and hit her in the shoulder. Wheeling, she charged at once, and Grizzly had time only to hit her over the head with the butt of his rifle. Then, as she reared over him, he stabbed her in the flank with his knife, at which she knocked him to the ground. Placing one huge, hairy paw on his head, she began to bite at his shoulder.

For a few seconds Grizzly lay still and played dead, hoping she would stop her attack. The cubs began to bawl, and the old bear turned to them, bleeding profusely. At that, Grizzly jumped up and drew his pistol. He did not fire, however, for he saw that the shaggy mother was dying. After a few moments she dropped.

Grizzly staggered toward her. It did not matter to him that he was torn and bleeding. He looked around for his companions, but they had disappeared. "Gray, Gray!" he shouted angrily. He wondered where he and Stanislaus were. In a moment he heard an answering halloo. "Where are you?" Grizzly demanded.

"I'm here," Gray answered from a clump of trees a hundred yards or more away.

"Do you expect to help me there?" Adams asked indignantly. He told Gray to come and help catch the cubs; he had already dealt with the old bear.

"Is she dead?" Gray asked cautiously, still at a distance.

"She's dead, but it was no coward that killed her," Grizzly exclaimed angrily as the other man approached.

Gray appeared abashed. "I thought you were gone this time," he admitted.

"It's only cowards who are *gone* in the hour of danger," Grizzly retorted. "You've acted in this affair like a miserable coyote." Gray flushed at the words, but said nothing. He knew that the rebuke was at least partly deserved.

When he saw Grizzly's wounds, he exclaimed at their severity. Grizzly shrugged impatiently. They were bad enough, but the cold water cure would soon make them right. He told his partner and Stanislaus to catch the two cubs, but soon became disgusted with their tactics. "You are more clumsy than cowardly; see the Old Hunter catch them," he cried. Dashing forward, he quickly seized one of the cubs and held it up. "See there!" he exclaimed. Heartened, Stanislaus chased after the other cub and soon caught it.

The young grizzlies, no more than a month or two old, were just beginning to cut their teeth. Grizzly later named one of them Funny Joe.[23] It became a companion second only to Ben Franklin and the Lady, and traveled to New York with Grizzly six years after its capture.

Grizzly's wounds soon healed, and it was not long after this adventure that they moved camp to Smith's Fork on the Bear River. There they sold meat and provisions to the westward bound emigrants. In early August, Gray announced that he was leaving. He had met friends at a nearby camp and would travel eastward with them, then head south to his beloved Mississippi. Finding that he couldn't dissuade him, Grizzly went with Gray to the trading post, where they settled their accounts as agreed—Adams to have two-thirds, and Gray one-third of the animals and profits. Adams kept two bears, two panther cubs, two fawns, and two wolf pups, as well as a pile of skins and hides and one thousand dollars in coin.

"He was a good hunter," Grizzly observed after bidding Gray goodby, "but like most hunters, not over fond of grizzly bears."

The next day, Grizzly pried up the bed of his wagon and cut a small square hole—a hiding place for his purse—in the axletree. Placing the purse with the cash in it inside the cavity, he covered it with tin and began to replace the wagon bed. As he worked, some curious passersby inquired what he was doing. The hole, they pointed out, was sure to weaken the axletree. Joking, Grizzly replied that he was making a hole in which to hoist a mast and a canvas sail. With that, he could sail over the prairies in his wheeled schooner without need for any team to pull it.[24] This answer brought many a strange look. Adams could see that the questioners thought he was crazy. He chuckled to himself.

The next day, he and the Indians headed for home, going the first lap by way of the Oregon Trail, from Fort Hall to Lewis's Fork. They did not reach their old campsite in California until October.

17

Trapping
the Giant Bear
Samson

Much to his dismay, Grizzly discovered that his camp had once again been destroyed—by fire this time—while he was away. Both the cabin and shed were burned to the ground; only the tools he had hidden in the cave were safe. During the next two weeks he and the two Indian boys rebuilt the cabin and shed, and harvested a winter supply of hay for the horses and mules.

Satisfied that all was in order, Grizzly returned to his hunting and trapping once more. He had received letters that fall from his contacts in South America, asking that he send them two large grizzly bears and one small one. He already had two bears that had been at Howard's Ranch all summer; it wasn't long before he trapped another one. Caging the three, he transported them to Stockton and sent them on their way.

Cold weather arrived, and snow soon covered the high and middle slopes of the mountains. One blustery winter morning Grizzly set out on a hunt, taking Lady Washing-

135

ton, Ben Franklin, and Rambler with him. Stanislaus and Tuolumne remained at camp. During the day, Grizzly bagged several deer, some rabbits and some quail. By late afternoon the weather had become increasingly stormy and windy, and snow had begun to fall. Grizzly reckoned that it was high time they started back; they were about five miles from camp, he thought. Packing the load of fresh venison on Lady Washington, he headed for home. Darkness fell during the next couple of hours, and a heavy snowstorm whirled about them. Grizzly could see no more than a few feet in front of him, and readily admitted to himself that they were lost.

Stumbling through the drifts, he and the animals eventually found a protected spot under a ledge of overhanging rock. Gathering some dead wood, Grizzly soon had a roaring blaze. Unpacking the venison from Lady Washington's back, he roasted a plentiful supply of meat to feed his pets and himself. Then all of them curled up to sleep. The storm continued, fiercer than ever, outside the opening of their natural cave.

When he woke the next morning, Grizzly discovered that deep snow, drifting down from the tableland above, had covered the opening of their shelter. After feeding the bears, the dog, and himself, he set about freeing them from their white prison. "Come on, Ben," he urged. "You've got big paws. Come and help me dig out." He, the bears, and Rambler worked at the wall of snow for several hours; Grizzly estimated that they dug a tunnel of one hundred feet or more before they broke out of the wind-piled drifts. Peering about, Grizzly saw that the storm had passed. He recognized where they were—some ten miles from camp.

The blizzard had left a blanket of snow that was much too

deep for them to travel through, so they remained in their shelter for the next five days. Grizzly packed in wood on Ben's back for the fire, and melted snow in wooden troughs for them to drink. During those five days, he also made crude snowshoes for the bears and himself. On the sixth day, they were able to make their way back to the cabin. Wintering in the Sierra Nevada had its problems, Grizzly admitted as he took up his regular routine of hunting and trapping.

One day he came upon bear tracks, the largest he had ever seen, in a ravine. Each huge hind footprint measured about a foot long and eight or more inches wide. He had seen more grizzly bears than anyone else around, he told himself, but none of them had tracks this big. He must capture this bear.

For several days he roamed the surrounding countryside, searching for either the beast or its den. He discovered a well-marked trail that the animal must have made, and finally came upon what he thought must be its den, deep in a narrow canyon close to the headwaters of the Tuolumne River. But he never glimpsed the bear itself.

Finding a good hiding place that overlooked the trail out of the canyon, Grizzly settled down to watch and wait. After several days, he finally saw his quarry.

To Grizzly, the great bear swinging down the path looked like a moving mountain. About five feet high at the shoulder and ten feet long, it probably weighed close to fifteen hundred pounds, Grizzly thought. The giant was light-colored, a uniform, grizzled gray-brown. It had a massive face and a thick shoulder hump. The face was broad and dished in, with shrewd little eyes that peered about confidently as the bear padded leisurely along the trail. This bear walked like a

The giant grizzly which Adams captured in the winter of
1854–55.

monarch, afraid of nothing in the mountains. Grizzly vowed
that he would capture it or perish in the attempt.

After the giant grizzly had passed, Adams went back to
camp to begin his preparations. He had already picked out a
spot high on a hillside near the approach to the den as a
good location for his trap. It was a place where, with a little
work, a wagon could be brought up, so the bear could be
hauled out in a cage after its capture. Together with Stanis-

laus and Tuolumne, he set to work felling trees and building the biggest bear trap he had ever made.

They first dug two deep troughs about six feet apart. Into each they placed a pine log some fourteen feet long and about two feet in diameter. To these, Adams attached cross-timbers that were fully a foot in diameter. The base of the trap was ready. On this massive foundation they built the walls, each log of which was the same size as those on the floor. The corners were locked together in the same way as a log cabin, and fastened with wooden pins and nails.

After the walls were built up to a height of six or seven feet, a flat top of similar-sized logs was added. The trap, almost as big as a small cabin, was fastened securely to two good-sized trees that stood close to it on one side.

Next, the sliding trapdoors had to be constructed, and a triggering device, the most delicate part of the whole structure, installed. An arrangement of chains and levers held the doors up until the bait inside the trap was disturbed. Then, if the triggering device had been properly set, the trap would be sprung and the heavy doors would come crashing down.

After a week of hard work, the giant bear trap was finished to Grizzly's satisfaction. He baited it with half a deer carcass, which he dragged behind the mule in a circle around the trap in order to spread the scent. Everything was ready. Would the great bear come into the trap?

A week passed, and Grizzly saw that Samson—as he had already named his quarry—had indeed visited the trap, and had even gone into it. For some reason, however, the doors had not dropped. Disgusted, he adjusted the triggering beams as delicately as he could and put out new bait. Day after day went by, and nothing happened. Hardly able to endure the suspense, Adams moved his base of operations closer to the trap. He set up a small tent a half-mile from it, and he and Tuolumne kept a nightly vigil. Every day they went over to check the trap and put out fresh bait. It was February now—the depths of the winter.

Two days went by, with no results. The third night, however, Grizzly was wakened by a terrible roaring and unearthly bellows that echoed through the hills and seemed to make the very earth tremble. Tuolumne was alarmed, and Grizzly had to calm him as he rose. He beckoned the other to come with him. "It's either the bear," he told Tuolumne, "or old Nick—and I guess it's not the latter."

Lighting torches, the two of them hastened toward the trap. Tuolumne, following behind Grizzly, was somewhat reassured by the rifle the trapper held ready, and by the fact that he himself carried a Tennessee rifle. As they got closer, the roaring sounded louder and louder. When they finally arrived, they saw that the giant bear was indeed in the trap, and doing its best to tear it apart. The great beast lunged at them as they peered at him through the logs. The whole trap shuddered, and splinters of wood flew out. Something had to be done quickly, Grizzly realized, or the bear might very well rip his way out.

Directing Tuolumne to gather firewood, he started a roaring bonfire—light by which they could watch the bear and reinforce the trap with additional logs and timbers. Tuolumne, understandably, was somewhat fearful of the whole situation, but Grizzly encouraged him as they worked to subdue the big bear. As often as Samson attacked the sides of the trap, Grizzly poked at him with an iron bar, or waved a torch in his face, to distract the bear from doing any additional damage to the log walls.

When he and Tuolumne had worked most of the night, Grizzly was satisfied that the trap was reasonably secure.

The huge grizzly did not give up, however. He kept up the fight, trying desperately to get out of his prison. "Then as it was absolutely necessary to subdue the temper of the beast, and make him feel man's superiority," Grizzly later related, "I commenced whipping him through the logs of his trap with a long iron crowbar, and, when he became outrageous, intimidating him with burning firebrands. Had I done otherwise, he would soon have torn the trap to pieces, or gnawed his way through."

At dawn, Grizzly sent Tuolumne back to the main camp to bring provisions, while he remained behind to watch over the captive. They kept up the vigil for eight days, for Grizzly was determined to subdue Samson, and the prisoner seemed just as determined not to be subdued. During this time, the big bear ate nothing except a few scraps of meat. He did stop his rampaging occasionally to drink the melted snow that Grizzly put into a small wooden trough through a hole in the bottom of the cage.

By the ninth day, Samson showed signs of surrender. He became quieter, and was seemingly resigned to his captive fate. Grizzly felt a great deal of satisfaction at this development; ". . . when they once succumb," he firmly believed, "they succumb (with occasional outbreaks) forever."

Samson remained in the log trap for nearly two months, guarded and looked after by Adams and his Indian helpers. Toward spring, Grizzly hired several lumbermen who were working nearby to feed and care for Samson while he and the boys left to take care of other business. He had moved to a new camp on the Merced River below Yosemite that winter, and soon headed for the settlements to get a cage built for Samson and hire a teamster and oxen to help haul the great bear out. Digging up his Rocky Mountain gold sack, which he had buried at the base of a pine tree, he made his way to Stockton. There, an old friend, a blacksmith, built him a strong cage with iron bars for one hundred dollars. He hired a teamster at five dollars a day, plus a yoke of oxen and a strong wagon at an additional five dollars a day, and a helper at three dollars a day. Together, they returned to the spot where Samson was imprisoned, felling trees to make a road as they went.

Samson had to be transferred from the bear trap into the cage. Lifted from the wagon, the cage was lashed to one end of the trap, and the doors between them removed. The bear may have been halfway subdued, as Grizzly believed, but he wasn't in any mood to leave the cage, even though he had been trying to get out for some weeks. No amount of poking or prodding or threatening him with firebrands could make him budge.

Grizzly had an alternate plan. Climbing on top of the trap, he cut a hole in it and, after much effort, got a loop of log chain around Samson's head, shoulder, and one leg. The other end of the chain was then snaked through the open door of the trap into the cage and out through the other end, where it was fastened to the team of oxen. He'd have the oxen pull the bear out by brute strength!

While Grizzly prodded the bear from behind, one of the other men urged on the oxen. Heaving with all their strength, they dragged Samson from the trap into the cage. The teamster, standing on top, dropped the cage door, and it was quickly locked.

After Samson had quieted down, the men took the wheels off one side of the wagon and boosted the cage onto its bed. Jacking up the wagon bed, they replaced the wheels, then paused to celebrate. Finally they started for Howard's

A team of oxen pull Samson from the huge log trap in which he had been imprisoned into a cage. This woodcut was made to illustrate an article in the New York Weekly *for May 31, 1860.*

Ranch. Grizzly had decided to leave Samson, together with some of his other animals, there for the summer while he headed out on his customary summer hunt.

It took them three days to reach the ranch, and along the way they met a number of miners and others who marveled at the sight of the great bear. But, as Grizzly sensed, many of them were "thinking me the queerest one of the lot."

18

Saved
by Ben
and Rambler

With Samson safely caged at Howard's Ranch for the summer, Grizzly made preparations for his summer hunt. Stanislaus and Tuolumne took their leave of Grizzly that spring and headed off for a visit with their people. The two faithful Indians were delighted with the farewell gifts that Grizzly gave them—a horse, one hundred dollars in gold coins, and a new suit of buckskins for each of them. They would be rich men in their tribe. They promised to return in a month, "but this was the last I ever saw of these two excellent boys," Grizzly recalled, "for in a few weeks after this time I removed from the region, and never returned, except for a few days at a time."

In their places, Grizzly hired a young man named Combe to look after camp for him. Together with Grizzly's favorite pets—Ben Franklin, Lady Washington, and Rambler—the two men set off for Corral Hollow in the Coast Range. Corral Hollow was a narrow valley about ten miles long; enclosed by mountains on either side, it was an area known for its California lions and other game. It lay in the shelter of Mount Diablo, which overlooked San Francisco Bay, and the road from San Francisco to Stockton ran through its bottomland. In this spring of 1855, there was great excitement over the discovery of gold in the Kern River area farther south, and the wagon road through the valley was much used by men heading for the new diggings. Adams saw the opportunity to make some money selling meat to the travelers, as well as trapping bears, panthers, and other wild animals. He made an agreement with a man named Wright, who helped run a small public house in the valley, to assist with the hunting and trapping. Soon they were doing a thriving meat business.

Much to Adams delight, Lady Washington gave birth to a cub at about this time, the fruit of her courtship with the wild grizzly in the Rocky Mountains. The cub thrived, and Grizzly named it Fremont, after the popular military leader and western explorer, John Charles Fremont. The bear grew up to accompany Grizzly to New York in 1860. He was, Adams noted, ". . . a bear of considerable intelligence and sagacity, though not equal in these respects either to his dam or to Ben Franklin."

Soon after setting up camp at Corral Hollow, Grizzly hitched up the mules to his wagon and headed back to his old campsite near the headwaters of the Stanislaus and Tuolumne Rivers, accompanied only by Ben Franklin and Rambler. He wanted to hunt in the old familiar haunts one last time, he said. Reaching the beloved camp, he settled down for a few days of hunting and glorying in the area he knew so well.

One morning Grizzly saddled a mule and set off with Ben and Rambler on a deer hunt. The morning was cold and foggy, and he rode through the mists for several hours before reaching one of his favorite hunting grounds. Hitching the mule to a tree, he started up a wooded valley to search for game, Ben and Rambler trailing behind him.

The sun finally appeared, and the weather warmed up. But there was no sign of deer. Grizzly was disgusted. Nothing to show, and soon it would be time to return to camp. He was descending a narrow ravine, following an old bear trail, when he heard a slight crackling in the chaparral beside him. Turning, he was chilled to see a big grizzly bear with three small cubs only a few feet from him. The old she-bear was standing on her hind feet and peering at him over the brush. After a moment she charged toward Adams, who struggled to put his rifle into position to fire and shouted desperately for help from Ben and Rambler. But it was too late—the enraged mother grizzly was upon him.

She swept the rifle from his grasp and knocked him down with one swift blow from her paw. That blow almost scalped him, too, for the long claws raked his head, tearing the skin and peeling it down over his eyes. The bear stood over him as he lay on the ground, and began to tear at his shoulders and back. This is the end, Grizzly thought. I'll never get out of this.

But, responding to his initial call for help, Ben Franklin and Rambler now pitched into the mother grizzly, Rambler attacking her flank, and Ben Franklin going for her throat. She immediately switched her attention to them. Feeling himself free of those tearing teeth and claws for the moment, Grizzly rolled over to where his rifle lay, and seized it. Wiping the blood from his eyes, he crawled to a nearby cedar tree and climbed a few feet upward.

The big bear had Ben Franklin down now, and was chewing at his neck while faithful Rambler, yelping with excitement, nipped at her heels and hind quarters.

THEY CAME TO MY RESCUE, AND PITCHED INTO
SHE-GRIZZLY NOBLY AND BRAVELY, THE DOG
ATTACKING HER IN THE REAR AND BEN IN FRONT.

Almost scalped by an enraged mother grizzly, Adams is rescued by his faithful companions, Ben Franklin and Rambler. Illustration for an article in the New York Weekly *for July 12, 1860.*

Ben, only a yearling and probably weighing no more than two hundred pounds, was getting the worst of it, for the old bear was much bigger and heavier than he was. Ben was roaring and growling defiantly, however, and so was the she-bear. The din was deafening!

Grizzly wiped the blood from his eyes again, and raised his rifle. His hand trembled so much, however, that he couldn't take good aim. He was afraid of hitting Ben. Taking a deep breath, he steadied himself and let out a loud shout. Snorting, the old bear looked around for her original enemy, giving Ben the chance to roll clear. Grizzly prayed as he took aim once more and pulled the trigger.

Screeching, the bear staggered, then dropped to the ground. The bullet had hit her in the chest—right through the heart, Grizzly thought. But she wasn't finished yet. She tried to get up to pursue the injured Ben.

Seeing that she was almost finished, Grizzly slipped down from the tree, knife in hand. Advancing slowly, he approached the old bear. She had sunk to the ground once more, and seemed unable to rise. Grizzly plunged his knife into her side half a dozen times, and the old bear died.

Looking about, Grizzly saw that Ben was running back toward camp as fast as he could go. The young bear was yelping with pain, and blood streamed from his head and shoulder. He appeared to be severely injured. Grizzly reflected that he himself wasn't in very good shape, either.

The mule was tethered about a quarter of a mile away. Plastering his torn scalp back from his eyes, Grizzly headed for the spot where he had left her. He crawled onto her back and headed her for home. He was weak from loss of blood.

When he got back to camp, he saw that Ben had crawled under the wagon, where he usually bedded down, and was licking his shoulder. He was bleeding from many wounds about his face and neck. Casting aside any thoughts of treating his own wounds first, Grizzly made his way over to his companion. His faithful pet was whimpering with pain. Grizzly coaxed him into the cabin, where he examined the extent of his wounds. He bathed and bandaged them as best he could, liberally dousing them with a concoction of medicinal herbs. Ben's skin was deeply torn about one eye, and the teeth of the she-grizzly had left terrible cuts on his shoulder, but Grizzly was confident that he would recover.

Only after he had treated Ben and made him as comfortable as he could did the hunter attend to his own wounds. His head felt as though it had been hit by a sledge hammer, and half his scalp still hung loose and bloody over his eye. Cleansing the torn scalp with water, he trimmed the ragged edges of skin and pushed the scalp back into its proper place as best he could. After dousing both his head and the wounds on his neck and shoulder with a healing liniment he had made up of snake root and blood root, he bandaged them.[25]

Over the next few days, he soaked both Ben's and his wounds at frequent intervals with the healing medicine and liberal applications of cold water. As always, he had great faith in the cold water cure, and it seemed to be working. None of the wounds became infected, and gradually they began to heal over. Both Grizzly and Ben were stiff and sore, however, and weak from loss of blood. Several weeks went by before either of them felt like hunting again. And both of them carried the scars of the encounter for the rest of their lives.

"That was one of the narrowest escapes I ever had in all my hunting," Grizzly Adams avowed several years later, "and, as my preservation was due to Ben, the circumstance explains, to some extent, the partiality I have felt toward that noble animal. He has born the scars of the combat upon his front ever since; and I take pride in pointing them out to persons who, I think, can appreciate my feelings toward him."

Of all his bears, Ben Franklin was Adams's favorite.

19

Adventures Along the Coast Range

Once they had recovered from their near brush with death, Grizzly and his pets returned to Corral Hollow. Adams had heard that the hills of southern California abounded with game, so he decided to head that way and spend the summer hunting and trapping in the Coast Range. Combe, his new camp helper, had no enthusiasm for such a trip, so, in his stead, Grizzly hired another young man by the name of Drury. Adams later recalled him as ". . . a smart enough boy, but very lazy, and shamefully fond of strong drink, as I soon learned to my cost."

Off they started, with two horses, two mules, and a wagon load of supplies and equipment, as well as Rambler, Ben Franklin, and Lady Washington. When they camped that first night, Drury pulled out the keg of whiskey while Grizzly was attending to other chores, and drank himself into a stupor. Enraged, Grizzly smashed in the top of the keg with an ax and poured the liquor on the ground. The next morning he indignantly upbraided Drury and threatened him with

151

instant dismissal if such a thing happened again, no matter where they might be. Then they started off once more.

As usual, Lady Washington was chained to the axletree of the wagon, while Ben and Rambler roamed free. Rambler had become an excellent hunting dog, and Ben had learned many of his foster brother's skills by example. As Adams remarked, "From an early period in the life of my bear, Ben Franklin, it had been my intention to teach him to be a hunter. I had therefore taken every means to cement the friendship which existed between him and the greyhound, Rambler; and so intimate had their relations become that they passed their time together by choice, always keeping in company in their plays."

Rambler enjoyed chasing pronghorn antelope, and could usually keep up with them for long distances. Ben would follow gamely, but his speed could not match that of either Rambler or the antelope. As Adams observed, ". . . he tried with all his might to keep up, but the further he went the more he fell behind." One day, he recalled, ". . . finding that his wind was giving out, he stopped, and came back with a look on his countenance, which showed that he did not wish to be considered as having been in the race." When Rambler finally returned, he ran to Ben and jumped about him, whining eagerly, as if to tell him what a great race he'd had.

Traveling leisurely, and stopping frequently to hunt, they made their way to Pacheco Pass, on the east side of the range. After two more days of travel over a rugged road, they came to the edge of a steep hill that overlooked the San Joaquin Valley, nearly one thousand feet beneath them. The slope was too steep for the horses to bring the wagon down behind them, so Grizzly and Drury unhitched the team and began to lower the wagon with drag ropes snubbed around trees. Lady Washington was still chained to the rear. In spite of all their efforts, the wagon overturned, and ". . . smash! over went the whole concern, tumbling and scattering the goods into the brush, overthrowing and crippling the mules, tearing the harness, twisting off the tire of one of the wheels, and breaking the tongue square off near the whipple-trees."

Lady Washington was pitched violently by the mishap, and her nose plowed a furrow in the ground. Shaken up and alarmed, she snorted with agitation, the hairs on her coat erect. Grizzly patted her and spoke reassuringly to comfort her. After a few moments she calmed down and licked Grizzly's hand, ". . . as if she understood the affair was only an accident and entirely unintentional."

When all their animals and equipment were collected at the bottom of the hill, Grizzly and Drury repaired the wagon and harness, repacked, and continued on their way. Dusk deepened to darkness, and the stars came out, clear and bright. Grizzly headed for a distant line of cottonwood trees which indicated a stream. When they reached the trees the next morning, however, they found that the streambed was completely dry.

All of them by now were beginning to suffer from thirst. Grizzly sent Drury ahead to search for water. His helper returned after an hour or more to report that he had discovered a spring—a pool under a cleft of rocks. When they reached it, Ben and Rambler plunged in eagerly to drink and roll and wallow. After all of the animals and men had drunk their fill and the animals had been fed, Grizzly and Drury rolled up in their blankets under the cottonwood trees and went to sleep. The hardships of the past twenty-four hours had exhausted men and beasts alike.

Grizzly awoke in late afternoon, refreshed by his sleep, and determined to push on immediately. While Drury hitched up, he went to the spring, where several antelope were drinking. He shot one of them for meat. As he began to skin the pronghorn, Ben came and sat watching him, begging for a bite. "The noble fellow was already so well trained that he never presumed to touch anything till I gave it to him, but he had a way of grumbling for food, when hungry, that was irresistible," Grizzly noted. "I shall never forget how he sat there, wistfully eyeing my carving . . . his patience at last assumed such a pitch, that he got excited, and grumbled more than ordinarily. I resolved to try him a little, and placed food in such a way as to tempt him; but the faithful fellow remained true to his training, and the meat remained inviolate. Seeing this, I threw his portion to him, and he ate until I almost thought he would burst . . ."

The next day they came to a beautiful valley where they camped to do some hunting. They bagged several grizzly bears and antelope during the next few days, and captured two young elk. Refreshed by the stop, they went on, leaving the valley and heading across a hot and sandy plain in the direction of the San Joaquin River.

After traveling some thirty miles across this harsh semi-desert, Ben began to show signs of serious exhaustion. He, the other animals, and the men as well, were becoming dehydrated. There was no sign of water anywhere near them, and only a faint line of trees some miles ahead indicated the place where the river might be.

Grizzly was quite worried about Ben's condition. The young bear was panting and wheezing noisily, and seemed to be in a bad way. Stopping, he sent Drury ahead on one of the horses to try to find water and fill their waterbags. He then attempted to coax Ben to head on too, but the bear's paws had become so sore and blistered that he lay down and refused to budge.

"The condition of my poor Ben, as he lay panting on the sand of the San Joaquin plains . . . grieved me to the heart, and gave me great uneasiness," Grizzly recalled. "He was my favorite; I could well have spared any other animals rather than Ben; and I feared he would die."

He fashioned a makeshift tent from a blanket as shade for his pet, and then left him while he drove on ahead with the wagon to get some water and bring it back for the bear as quickly as possible. He met Drury several miles ahead; his helper had found a spring and was returning with full waterbags.

Leaving the wagon with Drury, Grizzly hastened back to Ben with the water. The drink revived the young grizzly somewhat, but his feet were still too sore and blistered for him to walk. The only solution was to get him into the wagon. Leaving Ben once again, Grizzly hurried to the spring where Drury was waiting with the wagon. They started back, but got lost in the gathering darkness and couldn't find the place where Adams had left Ben under the makeshift tent. It was dawn before they finally spotted it. By then, Grizzly was almost frantic with worry.

Ben was lying as Grizzly had left him. Much to Grizzly's relief, he was still breathing. After giving him some water, he and Drury lifted the four-hundred-pound bear into the wagon and drove back to the spring. They camped there for two days while Grizzly doctored Ben's feet and nursed him back to health.

Once again, he made moccasins for his pet. After pouring bear's oil on them as salve, he bound the moccasins tightly to Ben's feet, and put a muzzle on him so that he couldn't tear them off. On the third day, they headed on.

They reached the Kern River after a few days, and Grizzly set to work hunting and supplying meat to the gold seekers. True to his nature, he tried his luck as a prospector too, but ". . . didn't get enough gold to put in a songbird's eye." He quickly returned to the work that he knew best.

One day he spotted an old grizzly with two cubs. Adams shot the old bear, and Ben and Rambler chased the two cubs. Although the young bears were ". . . nimble as crickets and wild as partridges," each of his animal companions seized a cub, and both were captured.

Pushing on south, they came to Tejon Pass, where the Coast Range and the Sierra Nevada join. In this area red or cinnamon bears—a color variation of the American black bear—were common. Grizzly was eager to get several of them for his menagerie, and when they finally encountered a mother bear with two young, Ben captured one of the cubs and Rambler the other.

Traveling farther south into the Tehapachi Mountains, Grizzly was wakened one night by the sound of the horses snorting. Seizing his rifle, he peered into the darkness, trying to see what had frightened them. There was no starlight, however, and he could not make out the source of the excitement. Then he heard sounds of lapping from the nearby spring, and saw "two spots, like balls of fire," glaring at him. The strange beast fled with a growl, and Grizzly glimpsed the retreating indistinct shape of a big cat of some kind. It looked bigger than any panther he had ever seen—about as big as an African lion, he thought.

The brief glimpse of this strange beast whetted not only his curiosity but also his love of adventure. "My imagination presented me," he recalled, "with the picture of an animal whose capture would exceed in interest all the adventures of my previous days."

He set out the next morning with Ben and Rambler to

explore the country and try to track down the mysterious animal. Late in the day they came to a rugged canyon, full of jumbled rocks. There he found the beast's den—a cave in a ledge of rock, the area around its entrance littered with bones.

Excited at having discovered the big cat's home, Grizzly decided to capture it by building a trap on the trail leading to the den. But since there were no trees in the area, he first had to search for timber. Several days later, he moved camp to a spot he found about ten miles from the den, a place with both grass and water—and the only sizeable trees for many miles in any direction. These would provide the necessary logs for building the trap. When the logs were cut, some of them ten feet long and six or eight inches in diameter, Grizzly used the horses and mules, and Lady Washington as well, to transport them to the place he had picked for the trap. The Lady dragged two big logs, one fastened to each side, on the long, uphill journey.

When they reached the site, Grizzly promptly set to work building the trap, while Drury returned to camp to bring back more timber. That night Grizzly heard the mysterious beast roaring, ". . . loud but clear, short but piercing, different from any roar I had ever heard."

After days of hard work, the trap was finished to Grizzly's satisfaction. Baiting it with meat, he then picked out a nearby hiding place where he could watch the den, the trail, and the trap. He settled down for the night with Ben, Rambler, and Lady Washington beside him, eager to see what might happen. Twilight faded into darkness, and Grizzly finally fell asleep.

Sometime later, he was wakened by a loud roar. Starting up, he peered in all directions, hoping to get a glimpse of the beast, but didn't see anything. The roar was soon repeated, and by the light of the new moon, Grizzly at last made out the figure of a big, spotted cat, "resembling a tiger in size and form." Beside her two cubs rolled about and played like domestic kittens. The animals soon disappeared into the

This largest of American cats, the jaguar, was seldom seen north of the Mexican border, even in Adams's day; the hunter tracked a family of them in the Tehapachi Mountains of southern California.

darkness. Adams could scarcely believe his eyes, but he realized that what he had been looking at were an adult jaguar and her young. Largest of all the New World cats, jaguars ranged from South America northward through Central America and Mexico, but were very seldom seen north of the border. To catch them would crown his animal-hunting career.[26]

Later that night he heard the roar of the male jaguar, and even heard the padding of its feet as it passed, but he did not see it. When daylight came, he observed that although the animals had passed close to the trap, they had not entered it.

Somewhat discouraged, he decided to try another method of catching them. After several days of backbreaking work, he and Drury dug a huge pit some eight feet long, six feet wide, and ten feet deep. They then constructed a door for it, "swung upon an axle in such a manner as to turn and drop any animal, that trod upon it, into the pit. The door was covered over with dirt, grass, and leaves in such a manner as to resemble the ground about it." When all was ready, Grizzly hung a large piece of bighorn sheep flesh over the door as bait. Finished, he returned to his hiding place to await results.

Soon after dark, he saw the entire family of jaguars—male, female, and the two cubs. The male looked at least twice the size of a cougar or mountain lion, and its coat, as Adams described, was "covered with dark round spots of great richness and beauty."

Grizzly's heart pounded as the family of cats approached the pit. They sniffed suspiciously, then carefully skirted it, much to his disappointment, and went on toward the trap. Again, they stopped to examine it. They even went in; but, for some reason, the falling door was not triggered. The jaguars came out and disappeared.

Adams used all of his skills during the next several weeks to trap the jaguars, but without success. He never saw the male again. He came upon the female and cubs one day, and having decided that he couldn't trap her, he fired at her. At the same time, Ben and Rambler bounded forward to engage her in battle. The mother jaguar gave them more than she received, however, ripping them with her teeth and claws before escaping with her cubs. Poor Ben once again was so torn and battered that Grizzly had to treat his wounds for more than a week.

By this time, fall and the rainy season were approaching. Despairing of capturing the jaguars, Adams reluctantly prepared to return north for the winter. Retracing his steps through Tejon Pass to the west side of the Coast Range, he and Drury headed for San Jose.

20

The California Menagerie

Grizzly had his usual share of adventures, as well as mishaps, during the trip northward into more settled territory. Drury, who had repeatedly shown himself to be incompetent during the summer, carelessly let the horses break away and join a band of wild mustangs; only the mules were left to haul the wagon. Then the wagon overturned on a steep hillside, scattering animals and gear. Shortly after that, the wagon became mired in soft riverbottom mud near the San Miguel Mission. The mission Indians and their Spanish masters trooped out to help pull it ashore—and to stare with lively curiosity at Ben Franklin, Lady Washington, and the other animals of the menagerie.

Adams soon realized that nearly everyone they encountered in these settled coastal areas was interested in seeing his animals. People everywhere crowded around to gawk at them. Often they brought food for the bears, or milk for the cubs, fawns, and elk calves. Although Ben and Rambler had been roaming free all summer, he was now forced to tie them

161

up, along with Lady Washington, because of the many dogs they met on the road. "This I did not for their own protection," he remarked, "as they could vanquish any number of dogs, but to prevent difficulties with dog fanciers, that irritable class of individuals, who are more often ready to fight for an effront to their puppies than for an insult to themselves."

One day, as they made their way along a steep hill beside a river, one of the mules balked. The wagon toppled over, falling against one of the mules and then down into the river, "making an almost perfect wreck, breaking the bed and tongue in several places, killing a young deer and elk, fracturing the leg of a small bear, and severely injuring one of the mules, which it dragged down with it. Here again," Adams noted, "was I the victim of misfortune; for it seemed truly as if only bad luck was in store for me."

In his usual resourceful way, however, he set about repairing the damage, and they soon continued the journey toward San Jose. Progress was slow, for one of the mules had been lamed in the accident. Upon reaching a ranch, they stopped for rest and recuperation. It was here that Adams and his pets had another encounter with a wild grizzly.

The rancher had been having trouble with a grizzly bear that was attacking his cattle. Leading Grizzly to a corral, he showed him the remains of a calf that the bear had killed just the night before. Adams realized, from the bear's prints, that it was a big one, and offered to kill it. He directed that the other stock be driven out of the corral, leaving only the body of the calf, and that all the ranch dogs be tied up. That evening he stationed himself, together with Ben and Rambler, behind a pile of logs near the corral. The night was clear and moonlit as he began his vigil.

About ten o'clock, Grizzly saw the calf killer approaching. He was a very big grizzly indeed. Clambering over the stockade walls, the bear began to feed on the carcass of the calf. Ben and Rambler were eager for a fight, and Grizzly had some difficulty restraining them. He wanted the killer to gorge himself; afterward, he might not be able to put up as much resistance as he normally would.

When he judged the time was right, Adams crept forward to the side of the corral. Taking aim at the big bear inside, he fired; at the same time he called Ben and Rambler, who immediately scaled the fence and began to attack the raider. In a moment all three animals were rolling in the dust, biting and tearing at one another. Adams managed another shot at the calf killer, but did not succeed in killing it. Indeed, it still showed plenty of fight. Seizing Rambler, the big grizzly began shaking him in its jaw, as the dog might have shaken a rat. Ben tried to defend his foster brother, but with little success. Then Adams vaulted the stockade and entered the fray, burying his knife in the wild grizzly's neck.

The bear immediately dropped Rambler and turned on the hunter. Ben kept up his own attack, however, and distracted the beast's attention long enough for Grizzly to stab it repeatedly behind the shoulder with his knife. After a few moments, the bear rolled over, dead.

"*Mucho bueno, Americano,*" the delighted Spanish ranch hands exclaimed when they saw the body of the big killer. Adams found himself "elevated into a personage of considerable importance among the rancheros of the neighborhood." After enjoying their goodwill and hospitality for a few days, he headed on to San Jose.

On reaching the city of San Jose, he began to exhibit his menagerie for individual entrance fees. He there added an eight-hundred-pound hog, the California State Champion, to his collection. He soon proceeded to Santa Clara, and from there to San Francisco. On September 23 he began to exhibit his animals, including some which he had retrieved from Howard's Ranch, in the basement of a building on Clay Street. He named his show "The Mountaineer Museum."

Advertisements for the show soon began to appear in San Francisco's *Daily Evening Bulletin,* and in early October a young reporter for the paper, Theodore H. Hittell, visited the museum. He was very interested in what he saw. "Descending the stairway, I found a remarkable spectacle. The basement was a large one but with a low ceiling, and dark and dingy in appearance. In the middle, chained to the floor, were two large grizzly bears, which proved to be Benjamin Franklin and Lady Washington. They were pacing restlessly in circles some ten feet in diameter. . . . not far off . . . were seven other bears, several of them young grizzlies, three or four black bears, and one cinnamon. Near the front of the apartment was an open stall, in which were haltered two large elks. Further back was a row of cages, containing cougars and other California animals. There were also a few eagles and other birds. At the rear, in a very large iron cage, was the monster grizzly, Samson."

After examining the menagerie, Hittell watched while Adams demonstrated his close relationship with Ben Franklin and Lady Washington. Grizzly put his hands around his pets' jaws and in their mouths, had them rear up on their hind legs and perform various tricks on order. He had them box and wrestle, and even jumped on Ben's back and rode around the room several times. Fascinated, Hittell began to write frequent newspaper articles about the museum.

Grizzly moved his "California Menagerie," as he now called his collection, to the California Exchange Building at the corner of Clay and Kearny Streets in December, and

reopened as the "Pacific Museum." He remained in this location for more than two years, showing his animals and
frequently adding new specimens to his collection. Soon he
hired a brass band that played every evening. By March of
1857 he had acquired a "sea leopard," probably a common
harbor seal, and a "golden bear." He raised the admission
fee to fifty cents as other additions followed in quick succession: a baboon, a vulture, three more grizzly bear cubs,
and a young sea lion.

Hittell was a strong supporter of Adams and his animals,
and promoted them through his stories in the *Bulletin.* As he
recalled years later, ". . . Adams lived among his animals.
He continued to wear buckskin; and when seen on the street,
it was almost always in his mountaineer garb. He slept, on a
buffalo robe or bearskin, in one corner of his exhibition room
or in a small adjoining chamber. He sometimes cooked his
own meals, but usually dined at a restaurant."

Grizzly Adams soon became a well-known feature of life
in San Francisco. He was frequently seen walking about in
his picturesque garb and followed, as described by one acquaintance, "by a troop of those monstrous beasts which
were entirely docile and oblivious to the crowds of children
and yelping dogs attending his passage along the streets."

In July, 1857, he began to relate his life and adventures to
Hittell in detail, for a book. "I told him plainly that I
wanted nothing except the truth," Hittell wrote, "and he assured me that he would give it. . . . His memory seemed remarkably good." Grizzly Adams did have a good memory
for details, and no doubt told the truth as he saw it. He
sometimes changed the details of a story, however, as he told
it to different people.[27]

During his years in San Francisco, he appeared on stage a
number of times, usually accompanied by one or more of his

bears. On November 2, 1856, he appeared at the Union Theatre or Hippodrome, as a featured performer with "Colonel Rowe's Pioneer Circus," which had opened just a few days before. Eager crowds came to see Grizzly and his bears in an act called "The Pony Races." He tried theatrical life again in January 1858, when he appeared at the Opera

Grizzly Adams parades through the streets of San Francisco with his bears. This illustration, from the collections of the California Historical Society, San Francisco, was made for a handbill published in 1858 by the printers and engravers depicted on the sign.

House. In August of the same year, the Lyceum Theatre featured him as "Yankee Adams."

On January 18, 1858, Ben Franklin, Adams's favorite bear, died of unknown causes. His passing was a bitter blow. Grizzly and Ben had shared many adventures, and Adams often told how the faithful bear had saved his life on at least one occasion, and had given him needed help on many other occasions. An obituary for Ben, probably written by Theodore Hittell, appeared in the *Evening Bulletin* the next day, under the heading:

DEATH OF A DISTINGUISHED NATIVE CALIFORNIAN

Ben Franklin, the grizzly bear, the favorite of the Museum man Adams, the companion for the last three or four years of his various expeditions in the mountains and his soujourns in the cities and towns of California, departed from this mortal existence on Sunday evening, at 10 o'clock. . . . The noble brute, which was captured at the headwaters of the Merced River in 1854, has been raised by his master from a cub, and during his life manifested the most indubitable indications of remarkable sagacity and affection. He was ever tame and gentle, and although possessed of the size and strength of a giant among brutes, was in disposition peaceful; rough, it is true, in his playfulness, but always well-disposed. He accompanied his master on hunting expeditions to the Rocky Mountains and through various portions of California, and on two occasions saved his life in long and desperate struggles with savage animals in the wilds. He frequently carried his master's pack, provisions and weapons; frequently shared his blanket and fed from the same loaf. . . . The old hunter would willingly have lost all the balance of his collection to have saved Ben. . . . His sagacious expression . . . and his great affectionate spirit are gone forever. Alas, poor brute!

Depressed by Ben's death, Adams experienced other hard blows in the months that followed. He was a poor businessman, as always, and began to be plagued by mounting debts. In May 1859, he was sued for overdue rent. In August, three months later, he moved his collections to the Pavilion Building, on the site of the present Lick House. Things would never be the same again, either for John "Grizzly" Adams or for his country.

That same month, oil was discovered in Titusville, Pennsylvania—a momentous event that would change the direction of the industrial revolution. Two months after that, abolitionist John Brown carried out his abortive raid on Harper's Ferry. The nation was in a turmoil as the storm clouds of the dispute over slavery and states' rights grew ever darker. The world was rapidly changing.

In January 1860, Adams packed his menagerie on the clipper ship *Golden Fleece* and set sail for New York and a meeting with Phineas T. Barnum.

21

Barnum
and
Broadway

Barnum had a big tent erected on a vacant lot at the corner of Broadway and Thirteenth Street to house the California Menagerie. There, as the *New York Clipper* noted, the "Old Hunter of '49" would be opening for business on April 30. "All sorts of animals seem to be comprised in the 'company', and those among our fellow citizens who are partial to 'roaring' amusements will doubtless be then on hand."

As advance promotion, Adams and his bears paraded down Broadway and back up the Bowery. A brass band led the procession, followed by a number of horse-drawn cages filled with wild animals. The feature attraction, however, was Grizzly Adams himself. He sat upon General Fremont's back as the big grizzly stood free and unchained on a wagon bed. On either side of him stood two other grizzlies, held only by chain leashes in the Wild Yankee's hand.

Stimulated by the parade, as well as the advertisements and articles in the newspapers, crowds flocked to see the show. Admission was a modest twenty-five cents for adults,

169

and just fifteen cents for children under ten. The menagerie was open to the public from ten o'clock in the morning until ten at night, and Grizzly Adams put his bears through their paces at intervals during the day, with feature shows at 11 AM, 3 PM, and 8 PM. Some bears danced and some sang, while others turned somersaults or wrestled with Adams. The audience reacted enthusiastically, but the real star of the show was Grizzly Adams himself. As one spectator recorded, "It's A-dams great show."

Grizzly enjoyed the limelight, and soon began a series of feature articles about his western adventures for the *New York Weekly*. He was in good spirits because of the success of the show, and few in the audiences would have realized that he was often suffering great pain from his old head injury, which Fremont had reopened.

Grizzly had not seen his wife, Cylena, for more than ten years, but she promptly came to New York from her home in Neponset, Massachusetts, to look after her husband. Barnum arranged for his physician, Dr. Johns, to come daily to dress the hunter's festering head wounds. The injuries were steadily draining Grizzly's strength, and the doctor told him frankly that he would never recover. The physician reported to Barnum, too, that Adams's broken skull would be the death of him in the not too distant future—a matter of weeks at best. Grizzly scoffed at such pessimistic talk. As Barnum had already noted, he had an "indomitable and extraordinary will."

Barnum also perceived that "Old Adams liked to astonish others, as he often did, with his astounding stories, but no one could astonish him; he had seen everything and knew everything." This attitude amused the master showman, for he shared such qualities himself. He thought it would be great fun to bamboozle Grizzly and put one over on him.

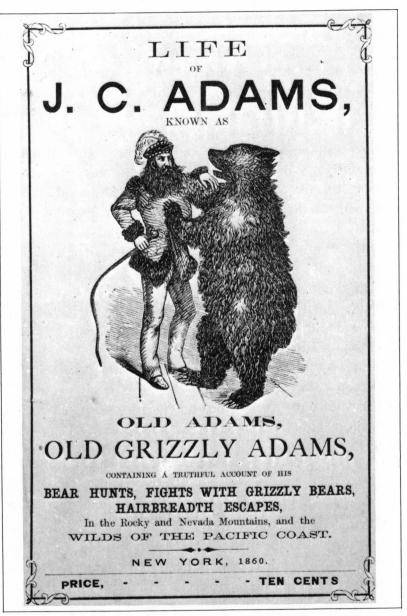

*Cover of 53-page pamphlet printed under Barnum's auspices in
1860 to promote Grizzly Adams's New York performances.*

The opportunity he had been looking for came one day when he purchased a pair of "golden pigeons." The plumage of these beautiful ruff-necked birds had been dyed a rich golden color by a special process. Barnum promptly put the birds into his "Happy Family" exhibit at the museum, and had them labeled, "Golden Pigeons from California." He knew that Adams was bound to notice them.

Sure enough. Several days later, Grizzly burst into Barnum's office. "Mr. Barnum," he said, "you must let me have those California pigeons. . . . All the birds and animals from California ought to be together. . . . You must lend me those pigeons."

"Mr. Adams, they are too rare and valuable a bird to be hawked about in that manner."

"Oh, don't be a fool," Adams snorted. "Rare bird indeed! Why, they are just as common in California as any other pigeon! I could have brought a hundred of them from San Francisco if I had thought of it."

"But why didn't you think of it?" Barnum asked.

"Because they are so common there," Grizzly avowed. "I did not think they would be any curiosity here."

Barnum chuckled inwardly at how Grizzly Adams had been fooled, and told him that he could use the pigeons in his California Menagerie. Adams went off, delighted.

A few weeks later, when Barnum was visiting the California Menagerie, he noted that the golden pigeons were molting. Many new white feathers were appearing among the yellow ones, and the birds looked quite mottled.

"Mr. Adams, I fear you will lose your Golden Pigeons; they must be very sick," he remarked. "I observe they are turning quite pale."

Adams glanced at the birds, then heard Barnum chuckle. He realized he'd been tricked. "Blast the Golden Pigeons!"

he exclaimed. "You had better take them back to the Museum. You can't humbug me with your painted pigeons!"

Seeing the vexed look of Adams's face, Barnum burst out laughing. He'd shown the old codger that he could be humbugged as well as anyone else.

Grizzly still had plenty of spunk and spirit, but he grew steadily weaker as the spring progressed. By the middle of June he was in such poor condition that Dr. Johns insisted he sell his animals and settle his affairs. He didn't have long to live.

"I'll live a good deal longer than you think," Grizzly said stubbornly. But he knew he was just putting up a front. Turning to Barnum, he said, "Well, Mr. Barnum, you must buy me out." Barnum agreed, and they quickly settled on the terms. Barnum had already made arrangements for exhibiting the California Menagerie with a circus that would tour Massachusetts and Connecticut that summer, and Adams insisted that he be hired at sixty-dollars a week, with expenses for his wife and himself, to travel with the circus and exhibit his bears for the season.

Barnum replied that he would be happy to engage him on such terms for as long as he could stand it, but also advised him to give up the show altogether and go home to rest. "You are growing weaker every day," he observed, "and at best cannot stand it more than a fortnight."

"What will you give me extra if I will travel and exhibit the bears every day for ten weeks?" Grizzly asked.

"Five hundred dollars," Barnum replied. He was certain that Grizzly could not last that long.

"Done!" Adams exclaimed. "I will do it, so draw up an agreement to that effect at once. But mind you, draw it payable to my wife, for I may be too weak to attend to business after the ten weeks are up, and if I perform my part of the contract, I want her to get the $500 without any trouble."

He watched while Barnum drew up the contract as they had agreed, and crowed triumphantly after Barnum handed it to him. "You have lost your $500!" Grizzly said, "for I'm bound to live and earn it."

"I hope you may with all my heart, and a hundred years more if you desire it," Barnum replied. He had seldom seen a man with so much courage and guts.

The ten-week tour—Nixon's Circus with the special added attraction of "Old Adams" and his performing bears—opened in Hartford, Connecticut on July 28, 1860. Two weeks later, Barnum went to see how his old partner was making out. He noted that Adams looked pale and weak, and judged that he was failing rapidly. But he tried to bolster his spirits.

"Well, Adams, you seem to stand it pretty well," he observed. "I hope you and your wife are comfortable."

"Yes," Grizzly replied, laughing. "And you may as well try to be comfortable, too, for your $500 is a goner."

"All right," Barnum replied. "I hope you will grow better every day."

Three weeks later, they met again in New Bedford. When Barnum saw Adams, he was convinced "that he could not live for more than a week, for his eyes were glassy and his hands trembled, but his pluck was as great as ever."

"This hot weather is pretty bad for me," Grizzly observed, "but my ten weeks are half expired, and I am good for your $500, and, probably, a month or two longer." In reply to this boast, Barnum offered to give Adams half the bonus if he would give up and go home. Grizzly scoffed at the idea.

During the next month, the California Menagerie sailed up the Hudson River on the barge *C. Vanderbilt*, stopping for performances at several cities and towns. On September 9, the barge was rammed by a lumber sloop near Troy, New York, as noted in the *New York Clipper*: "... everything above the Vanderbilt's guards, on the larboard side, from fore to aft was destroyed. Luckily, none of the artistes, two-legged or four-legged, the latter comprising grizzly bears and other animals, were injured in the least." On September 17 the show was at Newburgh, and on the 29th, it arrived at Newark, New Jersey.

The show arrived in Boston in early October, and there Barnum visited the Yankee hunter again. It was the ninth week of the tour, and Barnum saw at once that Grizzly was having a hard time. He was continuing to perform with his bears, however, even though he was now too weak to lead them into the ring. But he was still able to gloat over the fact that he was winning the $500 bet.

Barnum remained with him until the tenth week was finished. Then he handed Grizzly the $500, which Adams pocketed with high glee, remarking to Barnum that he was sorry he was a teetotaler as he'd like to stand treat. Then he turned to more serious matters.

"Mr. Barnum, I suppose you are going to give me this new hunting dress," he remarked, indicating the costume of beaver fur that he was wearing.[28]

"Oh, no," Barnum replied. "I got that for your successor, who will exhibit the bears tomorrow; besides, you have no possible use for it." Barnum had had the suit made for Herr Driesback, a noted animal trainer whom he had engaged to take over when Adams could not go on any longer. Seeing the suit, Adams had asked that he be allowed to use it temporarily, to wear on fair days when there was a large crowd to see the show.

"Now, don't be mean, but lend me the dress, if you won't

give it to me," Adams argued, "for I want to wear it home to my native village."

Barnum hesitated, but decided to humor his friend; in any case, Adams could not live much longer, and would be done with it. "Well, Adams," he replied, "I will lend you the dress, but you will send it back to me?"

"Yes, when I have done with it," Grizzly said, chuckling to himself. Then a new idea struck him. "Now, Barnum, you have made a good thing out of the California Menagerie, and so have I; but you will make a heap more. So if you won't give me this new hunter's dress, just draw up a little writing and sign it, saying that I may wear it until I have done with it."

Knowing that Grizzly could live only a few days more, at most, Barnum willingly drew up the agreement and signed it.

"Come, old Yankee," Adams remarked with a grin as he took the paper, "I've got you this time—see if I hain't!"

"All right, my dear fellow; the longer you live, the better I shall like it," Barnum said. The two showmen then parted with a warm handshake.

22
Silent Now
the Hunter Lays

Grizzly bade farewell to Barnum and to his beloved bears for the last time on October 19, and promptly returned with his wife, Cylena, to the family home in Neponset, Massachusetts. His daughters, Arabella and Arathusa Elizabeth, were twenty-one and seventeen; his son, Seymour, was fifteen. The family had managed, somehow, during Grizzly's long absence; their feelings about it are not recorded. We do know that Adams had sent money home from time to time while he was in California, and that Cylena had come to New York when he returned, to nurse and look after him.

Grizzly had few illusions about his accomplishments. In one of his last articles for the *New York Weekly,* published on February 18, 1861, three months after his death, the hunter waxed philosophical about "How I Came to be a Showman, with After Reflections."

"I have labored and made myself a slave to collect a menagerie of American animals, with a hope of enjoying the exhibition and realizing a fortune from it; but now I find

177

myself a slave to the thing designed to serve me, which does little else but exhibit me and demonstrate my own weaknesses and follies.

"Whatever course men pursue, it leads in the end to about the same results—satiety or disappointment. Some may succeed in winning fame, but a name is of little consequence when the head is bowed and the soul is sick. Few, I think, who have had much experience, are unwilling to bid the world a long good night when the summons [comes] for us to go up thither and leave the burdens of life behind us."

When Adams returned to Neponset, the threat of Civil War was beginning to sweep across the country. Abraham Lincoln would be elected President in just two and a half weeks; before the end of the year, South Carolina would secede from the Union.

Grizzly had little time left, however, to think about outside events. Once "home," he promptly took to his bed. His indomitable will and courage had sustained him so far. The challenge of his bears and the excitement of performances before enthusiastic audiences had kept him going. But now he had no such activities to look forward to. His faithful family surrounded him, but he was a helpless, bedridden invalid. How often he must have wished that he could spend his last days with his beloved grizzly bears in the glorious wilderness of the Sierra Nevada. He had voiced those sentiments to Hittell several years before: "If I could choose, I would wish, since it was my destiny to become a mountaineer and grizzly bear hunter of California, to finish my career in the Sierra Nevada. There would I fain lay down with the Lady, Ben, and Rambler at my side; there, surely, I could find rest through the long future, among the eternal rocks and evergreen pines."

On the fifth day after he came home, the doctor told John

This etching showing Grizzly Adams and his performing bears in New York in 1860 was made as an illustration for Barnum's autobiography.

Adams that he could not live until the next morning. Barnum, who recorded most of these details after conversations with Adams's family, noted that "He received the announcement in perfect calmness, and with the most apparent indifference." Turning to Cylena, he told her that he wanted to be buried in the beaver hunting suit he had gotten from Barnum.

"Barnum agreed to let me have it until I have done with

it," he asserted, "and I was determined to fix his flint this time. He shall never see that dress again." His faithful wife promised that he would indeed be buried in it, as requested. Satisfied, Grizzly then asked to see a clergyman, and spent more than an hour talking to him. As Barnum recorded, the hunter told the clergyman that ". . . though he had told some pretty good stories about his bears, he had always endeavored to do the straight thing between man and man. 'I have attended preaching every day, Sundays and all,' said he, 'for the last six years. Sometimes an old grizzly gave me the sermon, sometimes a panther; often it was the thunder and lightening [sic], the tempest, or the hurricane on the peaks of the Sierra Nevada, or in the gorges of the Rocky Mountains; but whatever preached to me, it always taught me the majesty of the Creator, and revealed to me the undying and unchanging love of our kind Father in heaven. Although I am a pretty rough customer,' continued the dying man, 'I fancy my heart is in about the right place, and look with confidence for that rest which I so much need, and which I have never enjoyed upon earth.' "

Within an hour he was gone—laid low at last by the head injuries inflicted by his beloved grizzlies, and by the subsequent infection and cancer which resulted. Barnum noted later that "It was said by those present, that his face lighted into a smile as the last breath escaped him, and that smile he carried into his grave. Almost his last words were: 'Won't Barnum open his eyes when he finds I have humbugged him by being buried in the new hunting dress?' That dress was indeed the shroud in which he was entombed."

Adams was buried in Charlton, Massachusetts, a small town some twenty miles west of Worcester. His final resting place was the Old Burying Ground, now called the Bay Path Cemetery, just south of the town common.

Harper's Weekly for November 10 noted the showman's passing with an obituary which briefly sketched his early life, his accomplishments in the western wilds, and how he had come to New York the spring before. "He had frequent personal encounters with his bears," it went on to say, "and after a time people began to feel a want of something in their personal paper if the chronicle narrated not how Old Adams had lost a leg, an arm, or a part of his head on the day before, through the petulance of his chief grizzly."

There is no record of what happened to Grizzly's wild friends. His favorite, Ben Franklin, died in San Francisco, but what of those companions he brought to New York: the faithful Lady Washington, the amiable and frolicsome Funny Joe, the sullen giant, Samson, the friendly but unpredictable Fremont, and all the others? What happened to Ben Franklin's faithful companion and tutor, Rambler the greyhound? Barnum wrote that the bears were added to the museum menagerie, under the direction of Herr Driesback, and were later sold to a company of showmen. Barnum did keep the huge sea lion, Old Neptune, however, and he was a great attraction at the museum.

Barnum's regard for his erstwhile partner was so great that he ordered at his own expense a tall gravestone for Grizzly's grave. It can be seen today. At its top is a carved picture of Grizzly in his hunting costume with a tame bear—perhaps Ben Franklin—beside him. Under this is the simple inscription:

JOHN ADAMS

DIED

OCTOBER 25, 1860

AGED 48 YEARS

Below is a six-line verse:

And silent now the hunter lays
Sleep on, brave tenant of the wild
Great Nature owns her simple child.
And Nature's God to whom alone,
The secret of the heart is known
In silence whispers that his work is done.

Afterword:
The Grizzly Bear
in History and Today

The story of Grizzly Adams is, in a way, also a chapter in the story of the big brown bears he had hunted and befriended during a crucial period in their history. In 1812, when John Adams was born, grizzly bears were almost unknown to most Americans. They were animals of the western wilderness, and except for a few hardy explorers and trappers, few white men had ever encountered them. The huge bears first became known to the general public through the journals of Lewis and Clark, who had many exciting encounters with them during their epochal journey of exploration through the western country, from 1804 to 1806. "The wonderful power of life which these animals possess renders them dreadful . . ." Meriwether Lewis recorded in his journal. ". . . we had rather encounter two Indians than meet a single brown bear." So impressed by such accounts was naturalist George Ord, who eventually described the grizzly bear and gave it its scientific name, that he called it *Ursus horribilis*— horrible or fearsome bear.

And fearsome the grizzly bear has always been. A big grizzly may weigh one thousand pounds or more, and stand eight or nine feet tall on its hind legs. Its mighty jaws and teeth are bone crushers. It has five-inch-long claws, and its huge paws can deliver blows like sledgehammers. Usually brown, the grizzly's fur may vary from almost white to nearly black in color. Light-tipped or grizzled hairs give it the frequent nickname "silvertip." The grizzly bear's huge size distinguishes it from the black bear, and so do the pronounced shoulder hump and the dished-in or concave face.

Universally respected as America's most dangerous big game animal, the grizzly is generally peaceloving. This is not always the case, however, as several fatal attacks in Glacier and Yellowstone National Parks attest. The bear's temper is highly uncertain, and its actions are unpredictable. The greatest peril comes from startling a grizzly, or stumbling unexpectedly upon a female with cubs. And more and more inexperienced vacationers are invading the grizzly's last few wilderness strongholds today.

In the early days, western fur trappers and mountain men knew the grizzly's temper and reactions only too well. Few men, however, ever had as many hand-to-claw encounters with grizzly bears, and no one ever mastered and tamed them as completely as John "Grizzly" Adams.

Before the coming of the white man, the grizzly bear ranged over most of western North America, from Alaska to the Sierra Madre Mountains of Mexico, and eastward as far as the Dakotas and Minnesota. Early mammalogists separated them into a number of species and many different races or subspecies. The California grizzly, averaging somewhat larger than the Rocky Mountain grizzlies, was considered a distinct race. Today, systematists consider the grizzlies, Alaskan brown bears, and the Old World brown bears, as races of one circumpolar species, *Ursus arctos.*

At the time of the Gold Rush, the California grizzly was abundant in that state. They preyed on settlers' sheep and cattle and ravaged their gardens. They were a constant threat to human beings as well, and miners and ranchers kept their weapons handy; they considered the big brown bears as 'varmints' and dangerous nuisances, and killed them whenever they had the opportunity. They ate grizzly steaks, rendered grizzly fat for oil and ointments, and made robes and rugs of grizzly pelts.

The brutal sport of bull-and-bear-baiting, which dated back to the early days of Spanish settlement in California, continued as a popular entertainment during the Gold Rush. It was eventually prohibited as California became more settled; but the killing of grizzly bears went on. By 1870 the big golden bears were rare everywhere in California, the "Bear Flag Republic."

By 1900, grizzlies had disappeared nearly everywhere in the state, with only a very few still roaming Yosemite and other Sierra strongholds. The last California grizzly was killed there in 1922; and the last ever seen in the state was recorded in Sequoia National Park in 1924.

The grizzly was disappearing throughout much of the rest of its range, too. Grizzlies vanished from Arizona and New Mexico about the same time they did in California. By the 1930s, they were gone nearly everywhere below the Canadian border, except for a few in pockets of wilderness in Wyoming, Montana, Idaho, and Colorado. A very few Mexican grizzlies still roamed the Sierra Madre of Chihuahua, but these vanished in the 1960s.

Today, the grizzly bear, *Ursus arctos horribilis,* still roams in the thousands through coastal Canada and parts of Alaska. South of Canada, there may be as many as eight hundred surviving grizzlies—some two hundred of them in the Yellowstone region of Wyoming, and perhaps that many in the Glacier National Park area of Montana.

The bears in these national parks are watched by park staff very closely. Individuals that show any aggressiveness or threatening behavior toward the ever-increasing influx of tourists are either killed, or drugged and transported to even more remote areas. Many people who camp in the grizzly's last wild strongholds in the parks believe that there is no place in North America for any animal that may pose a threat to their vacations. Many others say that the grizzlies were there first; they need and should have a few wilderness areas where they can roam undisturbed by people.

Notes

1. Built in Boston in 1855, the clipper ship *Golden Fleece* sailed from New York on July 14, 1859, and arrived in San Francisco on November 12, a voyage of one hundred eighteen days. On January 7, 1860, less than two months later, it sailed with Grizzly Adams and his California Menagerie, reaching New York in mid-April.

2. John Adams's roving nature may have come down to him from his great-great-great-great-grandfather, Henry Adams of Braintree, Massachusetts. That worthy ancestor brought his family from England to Boston in 1632, and was the founding father of the famous Adams family which included among its members Samuel Adams, the Revolutionary War patriot, two presidents of the United States, and a number of other eminent Americans.

John "Grizzly" Adams had seven brothers and sisters: Susan, Almy, Charles, James Capen, Zilpha, Francis, and Albert.

3. In 1833, at very nearly the same time that John Adams was felled by a tiger, Isaac Van Amburgh performed on the stage of the Richmond Hill Theatre in New York, entering a cage of assorted big cats—a lion, a tiger, a panther, and a leopard. He went on to international fame as a master of the big cats, and as a circus owner.

4. On May 17, 1849, a fire broke out on board the ship *White Cloud* along the St. Louis waterfront, the heart of the city's business district. Winds quickly spread the flames, which destroyed twenty-seven boats and their cargoes, plus three hundred buildings along the three-quarter mile section of the wharves. Total losses were five million dollars or more. Adams's cargo of boots and shoes were very likely destroyed in this catastrophe.

On June 5, 1849, less than three weeks after the great fire, John Adams's father hung himself. He may very well have invested his own life savings in John's venture, and become despondent when the footwear was destroyed.

5. The American settlers in California who revolted against Mexican rule in 1846 used a flag featuring a grizzly bear, a star, and a red stripe as their emblem of the California or "Bear Flag Republic." The same symbols are featured in California's state flag today.

6. Most of the Indian tribes which western settlers called "Diggers" lived in the Great Basin, east of the Sierra Nevada. They got that name from their habit of digging roots and tubers for food, and gathering acorns, nuts, and berries.

7. In interviews with his biographer, Theodore Hittell, in San Francisco, Adams maintained that his brother William had visited his camp in the spring of 1853, and that they had formed a partnership: William would finance his brother in collecting wild animals, and would arrange to sell and dispose of them. At least part of this story is fantasy. John had no brother William, and there is no evidence that any of his brothers traveled west during the period John was there. But Grizzly undoubtedly had business arrangements with someone to dispose of his animals for him— perhaps a circus agent.

In his publicity pamphlet written for Barnum in 1860, Adams stated that he delivered his bears to men named McSheer and Robinson in Stockton in 1853. These two may have been agents for Rowe and Company's Pioneer Circus, which arrived in California from Lima, Peru, in 1849, and played in San Francisco and a number of other California towns at various times between 1849 and 1857. It is quite possible—even probable—that Adams saw the circus in 1849, or shortly thereafter, and became acquainted with Rowe. In 1856, Grizzly appeared with some of his bears at the Union Theatre on Commercial Street, San Francisco. At that time this theatre served as a hippodrome for Rowe's Pioneer Circus.

8. Adams bought the land upon which his old camp was located from M. E. Duffield, for twenty-one hundred dollars, on March 7, 1853. The land, located between the Stanislaus and Tuolumne Rivers, was about sixteen miles east of Sonora, and just west of Pinecrest. The next year, a new road was built from Sonora as far as "Duffield's Ranch."

9. Howard's Ranch, where Grizzly boarded many of his captured animals, was in the San Joaquin Valley, some ten or twelve miles northwest of Mariposa, and less than half that distance from Hornitos. In the *New York Weekly* for July 19, 1860, Adams relates the story of Mrs. Howard's heroism when one of his big grizzly bears escaped from its cage and entered her kitchen. Taking refuge in the loft with her children, she coolly shot the bear and killed it. Afterward, she descended and continued preparing the evening meal for her husband and hired hands, who were working in the fields.

10. Adams told Hittell that his helper on the trip to Washington Territory was named Sykesey; in his 1860 publicity, he called the same man Saxon, or "Saxey."

11. Many Indian tribes lived in the regions through which Adams traveled during his trip to Washington Territory, and he was not entirely sure to which of them Chief Kennasket's tribe belonged. He said that "The tribe was one of those who flatten the heads of their children—a custom common to various nations—but I am at a loss whether to call them Nez Percés, Pend d'Oreilles, or some other name." None of the tribes actually flattened their children's heads. Their heads may have appeared flat on top, however, compared to the tapered heads of various tribes farther west, who sometimes did practice ornamental skull deformation.

12. At birth, a grizzly bear cub weighs from eight to eighteen ounces; at forty days, two to four pounds; at three months, five to eight pounds; and at six months, thirty to forty pounds. At nine months (its first winter) it may weigh from sixty to one hundred pounds; the following summer, when it is a year and a half old (the same age as Lady Washington when Adams captured her) it weighs roughly one hundred and fifty to two hundred pounds.

13. The location of Adams's summer camp in Washington Territory is never pinpointed, but Tracy Storer surmises that it may very well have been near Flathead Lake in what is now eastern Montana. This is east of the continental divide. In 1853, according to mammalogists, buffalo—which Adams hunted at this time—seldom ranged west of the continental divide in this area. Adams does mention, however, that the journey from his camp to Portland was about three hundred miles, which would locate him in Idaho.

14. Grizzly told Hittell that the name of his dead hunting companion was Foster, but in retelling the same story in the *New York Weekly* for June 14, 1860, he writes that John Kimball, his old companion on the Gila Trail, was the victim.

15. The name Yosemite means "Grizzly Bear," as noted by the 1869 guide book to the Yosemite Valley; it also notes that the Indian name for the region was Ahwahnee, which means "deep grassy valley in the heart of the sky mountains."

16. Panthers or mountain lions very seldom attack human beings. When sighted, they usually bound away.

17. Cold water was used by many doctors, and others, in the mid-nineteenth century, as a cure for all sorts of ailments and injuries. "Hydropathy," or "the water cure," used cold compresses for broken bones and almost anything else; it is still practiced in many places today.

18. A road from Sonora through the Sierra Nevada was opened in 1852, probably using the same route as that followed by explorer James Walker some twenty years before. At least five other passages for travelers were also opened through the Sierra in 1852, with attendant ferries across the rivers, toll bridges, and trading posts.

19. One of the foremost western pathfinders, Joseph Walker, blazed a trail from the Green River in present-day Wyoming to California in 1832. After skirting Great Salt Lake, his route followed the Humboldt River and Sink to Carson and Walker Lakes, and then crossed the Sierra Nevada, probably by way of the Tuolumne Canyon, to the Merced River.

20. Golgotha was the hill of Calvary, near Jerusalem, where Jesus Christ was crucified. The name comes from the Aramaic *gulgultha,* which means skull (the shape of the hill).

21. The Emigrant or Overland Trail stretched from Independence, Missouri, westward by way of the Platte and Snake River Valleys to the mouth of the Columbia River. In 1832 it became the main route to the Oregon country. In 1850 the eastern part of it became the route used by California-bound travelers, who usually headed south of Great Salt Lake and entered California via Walker's Trail, or several other possible routes. An estimated forty-five thousand emigrants headed for California in 1850 over this trail; fifty-two thousand in 1852; fifteen to twenty thousand in 1853 (most of these used the Sonora Road across the Sierra Nevada); and about twelve thousand in 1854. There were much fewer immigrants in 1855—a year of Indian troubles, when Lieutenant Grattan's force was wiped out by the Sioux near Fort Laramie, Wyoming.

Jim Bridger, one of the best known of all the mountain men, built his Fort Bridger in 1843 as a trading post for travelers on the Oregon Trail and California Trail. It was situated on Black's Fork of the Green River.

22. About twelve thousand Mormons left Illinois in 1846 to head westward. Brigham Young and his followers arrived at Great Salt Lake the next year, and the leader proclaimed this as the place to settle. In 1850 Young was appointed governor of the Utah Territory.

23. In his 1860 publicity pamphlets, Adams gave a somewhat different version of the capture of Funny Joe than the one he related to Hittell. In the later account, he tells of finding two cubs in the brush, seizing them and thrusting them into his shirt, where they remained when the mother bear attacked him. One of the cubs was crushed to death in the ensuing struggle; the other, Funny Joe, survived.

24. In his biography of Joseph Walker, Bil Gilbert notes that "An Independent [Missouri] resident who became known as Wind Wagon Thomas equipped a prairie schooner with a mast and sails." Thomas claimed that it would take people westward at a speed of fifteen miles an hour. The wind-driven wagon was wrecked, however, when it smashed in a ravine during a trial run.

25. In his account of this incident in the *New York Weekly*, Adams recalled that his Indian helpers, Stanislaus and Tuolumne, were still in camp; but, as he told it to Hittell, he and his pet bear were alone at camp.

26. The last jaguar reportedly killed in California was taken near Palm Springs in 1860. Very seldom seen since then north of the border, one of the big spotted cats was shot in southern Texas in 1946; another was taken in Arizona in 1949. Today the jaguar is rapidly vanishing throughout much of its range, and is classified as an endangered species.

27. Grizzly's real name was John Adams; why he usually did not use it remains a mystery. When Theodore Hittell first interviewed him in October, 1856, Adams evidently told the reporter that his name was William. After a few days, he switched to calling himself James Capen Adams—the name Hittell used in his biography (Capen was his mother's maiden name). John did have a younger brother whose name was James Capen Adams.

28. The worn buckskin outfit which Adams wore most of the time when he showed his California Menagerie in New York and on the New England tour is preserved at the Worcester, Massachusetts, Historical Society.

Acknowledgments

I first became aware of Grizzly Adams and his exploits many years ago, when I was engaged in research on another project. Since then, I have read everything I could about his life and times, and explored every lead I could uncover. Many of those leads were blind alleys, but the search itself has been fascinating.

One of the main difficulties has been to try to separate the truth about John Adams from the legends and tall stories that grew up around him while he was alive, and which multiplied after his death through dime novels and similar publications. More recently, a movie and a television series about Grizzly Adams portrayed him as a peaceful and rather saintly mountain man who befriended all the animals about him and seldom ate meat or wore animal skins—a very different character from the real man. The adventures of the movie and TV hero were fictional, too, the major similarity with the real Grizzly Adams being that both had a pet grizzly named Ben.

Many of the stories that were published about Grizzly Adams during his lifetime were either written by Adams himself, or related by him to writers who interviewed him. Sometimes he told somewhat different versions of the same adventure to different people, as I have noted in this account of his life.

* * *

I gratefully acknowledge my indebtedness to all those who have written about the real John "Grizzly" Adams—including Adams himself. I owe a great deal to Theodore H. Hittell's biography, written after extended interviews over many months, and first published in 1860. This is the most detailed account of Grizzly's western adventures, and the author carefully checked the truth of Adams's story, as far as possible. Many of the quotes in this book are taken from this source. Phineas T. Barnum's autobiography has also been valuable for its details of Adams's activities in New York and New England in 1860, and I thank Alfred A. Knopf, Inc. for permission to quote from their 1927 edition of Barnum's life. Information was also sifted from two publicity pamphlets published in 1860, purportedly written by Adams himself, and from the series of articles which Grizzly wrote that same year for the *New York Weekly*. Two much more recent books, Richard Dillon's *The Legend of Grizzly Adams* (1966), and *The California Grizzly* (1955) by Tracy Storer and Lloyd Tevis are reliable checks on many aspects of Grizzly's life, and were especially valuable to me in pinpointing various geographical locations as uncovered by modern research.

Fifteen years ago, the late Emily W. McLeod, then editor of children's books at Atlantic Monthly Press, advised and encouraged me in the early stages of my research, and I wish to acknowledge her help. Many librarians, curators, and individuals too numerous to list have been helpful and cooperative through the years as I sought specific information. Particular thanks go to Eleanor W. Pellissier, former Town Clerk at Charlton, Massachusetts; Edith Maynard, of the Worcester Historical Society; Mrs. Fred C. Harrington, Jr., Librarian of the Missouri Historical Society; and to the many librarians who have helped me during the course of my research the past two years at the Amherst Town Library, the Robert Frost Library at Amherst College, the Morrill Science Library at the University of Massachusetts, and the Forbes Library in Northampton, Massachusetts.

Bibliography

The principal books and other publications that either deal directly with the life of Grizzly Adams, or give particularly valuable background material about the places and period in which he lived, are listed below. Many notices and advertisements for Adams's shows appeared in various newspapers, especially the San Francisco *Daily Evening Bulletin,* from September 23, 1856 through December, 1859; and the *New York Clipper,* from April 28, 1860 through September 29, 1860.

ADAMS, ANDREW N. *A Geneological History of Henry Adams of Braintree, Mass., and His Descendants; also James Adams, of Cambridge, Mass., 1632–1897.* Rutland, Vermont: The Tuttle Company, 1898.

ADAMS, J. C. [GRIZZLY ADAMS]. *Life of J. C. Adams, known as Old Adams, Old Grizzly Adams, containing a truthful account of his Bear Hunts, Fights with Grizzly Bears, Hairbreadth Escapes, in the Rocky and Nevada Mountains, and in the Wilds of the Pacific Coast.* New York: 1860. Fifty-three-page pamphlet, purportedly "Written by Himself" after he joined P. T. Barnum.

ADAMS, J. C. *The Hair-Breadth Escapes and Adventures of 'Grizzly Adams' in Catching and Conquering the Wild Animals included in his California Menagerie.* New York: 1860. Twenty-nine-page pamphlet written as above.

ADAMS, J. C. "Wild Sports in the Far West." *New York Weekly*. A series of articles published at irregular intervals from May 31, 1860 until July 13, 1861. The May 24, 1860 issue carried an "Announcement that J. C. Adams, better known as 'Grizzly Adams,' the Old California Trapper of '49 will write a series exclusively for the *New York Weekly."* The articles appeared as follows:

1. How I Captured the Grizzly Bear, Samson. (May 31, 1860).
2. How I Captured the Grizzly Bear, "Funny Joe." (June 7, 1860).
3. A Dead Companion and a Hunter's Funeral. (June 14, 1860).
4. A Deer Hunt and its Consequences. (June 21, 1860).
4. [5] Chased by a Grizzly—Can a Man Run as Fast as a Bear? (June 28, 1860).
5. [6] Exploring a Cave—Unpleasant Meeting with a California Tiger. (July 5, 1860).
7. How I was Scalped by a She Grizzly. (July 12, 1860).
8. A True Heroine—A Huge He-Grizzly in the Kitchen—How the Wife and Two Children Escape and Kill the Grizzly. (July 19, 1860).
9. A Night with an Old "Brave"—His Terrible Encounter with a Wounded Grizzly. (July 26, 1860).
9. [10] A Snow Storm in the Mountains—Five Days Life Under A Snow Drift. (August 2, 1860).
11. Hunting Sea Lions. (August 9, 1860).
12. An Attack of Gold Fever—The Cure—How I Capture Two Golden Bears by Approaching Nature on the Blind Side (September 27, 1860).
13. I Start for Correll Hollow—Fever and Ague Attacks Me on the Road, and is Put to Flight By the Spanish Remedy—the Horrors of a Night Followed by a Beautiful Morning. (October 4, 1860).
14. My Strange Companions—Pursuing a Grizzly—Grizzly Returns the Compliment—a Jump for Life. (December 28, 1860).
[15.] How I Made Several Additions to my Menagerie and How I Came to Be a Showman, with After Reflections. (February 28, 1861).
[16.] How I Got Under a Cloud, and What Came of It—Reject an Offer of Marriage from a Queen. (August 13, 1861).

BARNUM, PHINEAS T. *Struggles and Triumphs, or Forty Years Recollections of P. T. Barnum. Written by Himself.* Two volumes. Edited, with introduction by George S. Bryan. New York: Alfred A. Knopf, 1927. This is the same book, with revisions by Barnum, as *Life of P. T. Barnum, Written by Himself*, published in 1855, with reprints and new editions until 1890.

BILLINGTON, RAY ALLEN. *The Far Western Frontier, 1830–1860.* New York: Harper & Brothers, 1956.

BORTHWICK, J. D. *Three Years in California* [1851–53]. Edinborough, Scotland, 1857. Reprinted as *The Gold Hunters, A First Hand Picture of Life in California Mining Camps in the Early Fifties.* Cleveland/New York: The MacMillan Company, 1917. Also reprinted by California Biobooks, 1948.

DILLON, RICHARD. *The Legend of Grizzly Adams: California's Greatest Mountain Man.* New York: Coward-McCann, Inc., 1966.

DURANT, JOHN AND ALICE. *Pictorial History of the American Circus.* New York: A. S. Barnes and Company, Inc., 1957.

FARQUHAR, FRANCIS P. "The Grizzly Bear Hunter of California." A bibliographical essay included in *Essays for Henry R. Wagner.* San Francisco: The Grabhorn Press, 1947.

GILBERT, BIL. *Westering Man. The Life of Joseph Walker, Master of the Frontier.* New York: Atheneum Press, 1983.

HITTELL, THEODORE H. *The Adventures of James Capen Adams, Mountaineer and Grizzly Bear Hunter of California.* San Francisco: Towne and Bacon, 1860; and Boston: Crosby, Nichols, Lee and Co., 1860. Charles Scribner's Sons published a new edition in 1911, with an introduction and postscript added by the author; it was reprinted in 1912 and 1926.

MARRYAT, FRANK. *Mountains and Molehills, or Recollections of a Burnt Journal.* New York: Harper and Brothers, Publishers, 1855. This has been reprinted in facsimile from the first American edition by the Stanford University Press, in 1952.

MURRAY, MARION. *Circus! From Rome to Ringling.* New York: Appleton-Century-Crofts, Inc., 1956.

PERKINS, WILLIAM. *Three Years in California: William Perkins' Journal of Life at Sonora, 1849–1852.* Berkeley and Los Angeles: University of California Press, 1964. With an introduction and annotations by Dale S. Morgan and James R. Scobie.

STORER, TRACY I. AND TEVIS, LLOYD P. JR. *California Grizzly.* Berkeley: University of California Press, 1955. Now available in paperback from the University of Nebraska Press, Lincoln.

Index

Illustrations in **boldface.**